D0458675

PEOPLE
STRATEGY

JACK ALTMAN

PEOPLE
STRATEGY

HOW TO INVEST IN PEOPLE AND

MAKE CULTURE

YOUR COMPETITIVE ADVANTAGE

WILEY

Published by John Wiley & Sons, Inc., Hoboken, New Jersey.
Published simultaneously in Canada.

For general information on our other products and services or for technical support, please contact our Customer Care Department within the United States at (800) 762-2974, outside the United States at (317) 572-3993 or fax (317) 572-4002.

Wiley publishes in a variety of print and electronic formats and by print-on-demand. Some material included with standard print versions of this book may not be included in e-books or in print-on-demand. If this book refers to media such as a CD or DVD that is not included in the version you purchased, you may download this material at http://booksupport.wiley.com. For more information about Wiley products, visit www.wiley.com.

Library of Congress Cataloging-in-Publication Data is Available:
ISBN 9781119717041 (Hardcover)
ISBN 9781119717058 (ePDF)
ISBN 9781119716945 (ePub)

Cover Design and Images: Luc Chaissac/Lattice

SKY10026458_042121

To my wife, Julia, and my son, Liam

Contents

Introduction: Why Your Company Should Put People First

In early 2015, I experienced something of a professional crisis. The company I had worked for and loved for more than two years seemed to have lost its magic. It had quickly grown from a plucky start-up, with a vibrant company culture and clearly defined roles, to a stifling environment that was wrought with tension and a crippling lack of trust.

I remember while sitting at my desk one day, I just looked around the office and thought to myself, "What happened?"

To understand where it went wrong, we have to go back a few years. In 2013, I packed my bags, bid farewell to my 600-square-foot Manhattan apartment, and headed out to San Francisco to join this fledgling start-up. I suppose that you could describe it as risky, but I knew this company quite well. I'd been working from New York as an early-stage start-up investor, and Teespring (https://teespring.com/) was one of the companies in which I'd invested. I strongly believed that the founders and the business were brimming with potential.

My early days at Teespring represented the best of what's possible for a company culture. For one thing, we had a clear sense of purpose that was uniformly shared; we existed to help Internet creators make businesses out of their passions. We all knew what we wanted to accomplish as a company, why that would be valuable to the world, and what our roles were in making that a reality.

Another cornerstone of our culture was that we were all learning and growing at a rapid pace. Because the company was evolving so quickly, we were all constantly being thrown into new situations and we were determined to figure them out. As a result, most of us were improving our crafts and broadening our knowledge faster than at any other point in our careers. This was extremely gratifying and engaging, which created a virtuous cycle: invest more, learn more, feel great, be motivated to invest more, and so on.

Finally, because of our clear mission, shared values, and full engagement in our work, we built incredibly close friendships and a strong collective community. This too had a self-reinforcing dynamic, where our care for one another led to deeper investment in our work and vice versa. Even today, nearly eight years later, I am still friends with many of those early colleagues from Teespring.

Somewhere along the way, however, this company which my teammates and I held so dear took a bad turn. The culture shifted from one of clarity, optimism, and community to one of scattered priorities, fear, and territorialism. Our executive team meetings, which had once been focused on solving our most important problems, became full of interpersonal tension and disagreements about important strategic issues. Teams across the company became more siloed, and their connections became increasingly tenuous. We underinvested in HR and people management practices, so people didn't have clear goals or expectations, feedback was irregular or nonexistent, and the company didn't do enough to understand how its employees were feeling so that we could make course corrections.

In short, our culture lost its way. It was against this backdrop that the idea for Lattice was born (https://lattice.com/).

Eric Koslow was another early Teespring employee (he'll remind anyone who will listen that he was just a little bit earlier than me), and he and I had become good friends. Eric was Teespring's lead engineer, but he was also an astute observer of business dynamics and company culture. He also shared my love for what Teespring *used* to be and my pain over the direction things had been heading.

One of our favorite extracurricular activities was "exercising" together. I say exercise in quotes because we'd meet in the gym, and over the course of 90 minutes, maybe do 5 minutes' worth of exercise and 85 minutes' worth of talking. This time away from our phones and with the extra mental acuity from vague physical activity was a perfect breeding ground for countless start-up ideas. Eventually, we realized that the problem that we cared about most, and had some ideas for how to solve, was company culture and people management.

In the summer of 2015, we incorporated Lattice. We aimed not to just get back that feeling of clear mission, shared values, and passionate engagement in our work in a company that was our own. We also wanted to build a product that would help other companies invest deeply in people and culture that would make their companies the best places to work.

We also got the opportunity to try to build a company culture of our own that reflects the change that we were trying to see in the world. We believe that community, purpose, and growth are central pillars of a meaningful work experience, and so that is what we've tried to weave into the fabric of what it means to work at Lattice. And those pillars, we would later understand, are also at the heart of smart people strategy.

As I write this in 2020, I feel grateful that Lattice has been lucky enough to employ hundreds of people, serve thousands of customers, and raise about $100 million in venture capital. We've been able not only to ride but also to help *shape* the new wave of HR software and people practices.

Our first few years at Lattice were relatively smooth sailing; we grew steadily and evolved our product. But after a year of incredible growth in 2019 – revenue grew by nearly 200 percent, our team grew from 50 to 125, and we raised two new rounds of financing – the COVID-19 pandemic hit us and everything changed, literally overnight.

One morning in early March 2020, we awoke to a flurry of messages in our company chat tool Slack: early birds arriving at the office learned that the building was closed because a member of the building's janitorial staff had been on a cruise ship where many passengers had tested positive for COVID-19. As a result, the building would be closed for the rest of the week.

It was a chaotic day, but the company was good-natured, supportive of each other, and found their footing relatively quickly. I remember people making jokes in Slack, sharing articles about best practices for working from home, and posting pictures of their new makeshift home office setups.

By the following Wednesday, March 11, the tone of the whole thing changed. The spread of the coronavirus had already been very real in other parts of the world, but this was the day that it became very real in the United States, even though the country only had 1,000 reported cases. The World Health Organization declared the disease a global pandemic. The Dow Jones fell by almost 1,500 points. The first case of the virus was reported on Capitol Hill. A professional basketball player tested positive, and the NBA became the first major sports league to announce that there would no longer be fans at their games. That night, President Trump addressed the country from the Oval Office, and announced a travel ban with Europe. As we went to bed that night with our heads spinning, actors Tom Hanks and Rita Wilson shared that they, too, had contracted the virus.

The next few weeks presented an incredible challenge for Lattice, as they did for so many others around the world. As each day went by, we began to realize more fully and accept the reality that the world wasn't just going to return to normal, and that we'd need to settle in for a bumpy ride.

Our customers were also reeling as they scrambled to adjust to working from home and to make sense of what this all meant for them. The economy started to free-fall, with the stock market plummeting and unemployment claims going through the roof.

Lattice's business ground to a halt. HR software budgets got slashed, sales cycles slowed to a snail's pace as people focused on more pressing issues, and every day brought news of more and more layoffs. We'd been planning for hyper growth, and instead we were looking at a much different reality with no sign of when it would let up. Although the company's spirits remained surprisingly high, our numbers were telling a different story. Revenue growth went from lightspeed to glacial; cash burn went from manageable to high, and customer churn became a real concern. Our leadership team was worried. I wasn't sleeping well.

As April dragged on, the numbers told a grim story, and I was faced with a decision I hope never to have to face again: do I keep waiting to see more data and hope that the economy has a quick recovery, or do I swallow the bitter pill of a layoff and let go of people from sales and customer success to reflect the new pace of business and reduce our costs?

After weeks of deliberation, on the night of my 31st birthday, I made the decision to go ahead with a layoff. An hour after making that excruciating decision, I hopped on a surprise video chat with a couple dozen friends and family that my wife Julia had set up, but I didn't feel much like celebrating.

Two weeks later, we went through with the reduction-in-force, parting ways with about 10 percent of our team. Delivering the news to the entire staff was the worst moment of my professional career – made worse by the awkwardness of having to deliver it over video chat – and I barely kept it together as I explained to the company why I felt we had to do this. We gave generous severance packages and support, and we used our resources to ease the transition for those who were impacted as much as we could.

It was gut-wrenching, and I was fully expecting anger and outrage. But I watched in wonder as the company instead turned to positivity and supportiveness on this incredibly difficult day. As we met individually with the team members we were laying off, they told us how much they loved the company and that we shouldn't be too hard on ourselves for the difficult choice we had made. In a goodbye Slack channel, the departing employees shared well wishes and memories, and the rest of the company reacted and responded with love and care. The managers who needed to let go of employees through no fault of their own did so with focus, care, and respect. I was so completely taken aback by the outpouring of graciousness, understanding, and humanity, that when the day was finally over, I didn't know what to do but sit down, cry.

Despite the incredible difficulty of this time, it renewed my conviction in the importance of a healthy company culture. It's easy to have happy employees when things are going well, but you get tested when things get hard, which they inevitably do for all companies.

So, the question becomes how does your company culture show up in those moments? Do people resort to fear, anxiety, and inward focus, or do they choose hope, a sense of purpose, and a focus on the greater good? Do tough times break your culture down, or do they catalyze increased strength and solidarity? And how can you intentionally build a culture that helps your company stand up when others might fall down?

Tough as this period was, in so many ways, we came out stronger. Relationships strengthened, our purpose in the world was further clarified, and our values shone through while so much else fell into the background. I was reminded of why we started Lattice in the first place. We built it to help companies build culture off an intentional system of principles – a framework for people strategy.

This book is about people strategy; the set of practices that determine how you attract, retain, and grow your employees in order to best accomplish your company's mission. Most companies have clear product and go-to-market strategies that are deeply contemplated, debated, and refined over the years and are customized based on the particularities of the market in which the company exists. But when it comes to a strategy for our companies' people, who are the foundation upon which all other business strategies are predicated, things get very murky or nonexistent quickly.

Ask yourself this: you wouldn't go into your annual planning stage without a sales strategy or a marketing strategy or a product strategy, so why would you go forward without a people strategy?

Over the years, through building our own company and seeing thousands of our customers work through their people management on our platform, we've learned about what it means to be a *people-centric company*: a company that believes that people are at the center of everything they do, and what it takes to really be such a company. We've learned about the nuts and bolts of performance management, employee engagement, career development, hiring, and more, and our goal with this book is to share those learnings with a broader audience so that they can incorporate them into their companies, too.

While I started writing this book before the COVID-19 pandemic severely impacted the economy, at a time when companies were experiencing dizzying levels of growth and the war for talent made being "people-centric" imperative for recruiting and retaining employees, we actually believe that these pillars of people strategy matter now more than ever. Your people are your competitive advantage, particularly when you have smaller teams with shifting and steep goals. Knowing who are your top performers, keeping them engaged, and growing them up with the business is key to company success.

In this book, I will share the principles of people strategy and how to apply them to your business. We will discuss how a people-centric approach can help your business find its north star in the form of company values, the bedrock of organizational culture, and how those can help guide you with smarter hiring. We'll look at how leading "people first" can help managers lean into a culture of feedback that will improve performance and help employees feel heard. We'll show how employee engagement is a key central focus of the strongest, most enviable company cultures (the one I wanted back when I knew that Teespring had lost its way). And finally, we'll show how growing and developing your people's career paths will keep your strongest performers with you longer.

Throughout, you will gain insight from some of the brightest minds in business, including Marc Benioff, Greenhouse CEO Daniel Chait, and HR leaders from companies like Anaplan, Webflow, and Asana. In the end, I hope to show you how a people-centric approach is not just beneficial for the employees – a company's most important asset – but for the business, as well.

1

The Three Pillars
of Company Culture

Before we get too far along, I want to spend a little time clarifying what I mean when I talk about culture and explain why it's such a critical component of People Strategy.

So, what is culture? Culture is the summation of all the thousands of interactions, norms, and behaviors at a company. Culture is also the vehicle through which employees can attain a meaningful work experience.

Over the years for many of us, our relationship with our work has changed for the better. Our teams today have very different needs and expectations of their leaders and of companies than those in previous decades. We no longer want companies simply to provide us with something to do for five days out of every week and give us a paycheck. We want them to help us grow and align with our beliefs and causes. This has only become more pronounced as cultural headwinds, such as the coronavirus pandemic, force many to transition into remote work settings.

The Reason You Get Out of Bed in the Morning

Through my work with thousands of customers and hundreds of employees, I've observed that most people look for three key attributes to be truly dedicated and engaged in their work: **purpose**, **community**, and **growth**. These are the three pillars that serve as the foundation of a strong company culture (see Figure 1.1). Ideally, each of these elements is strong all the time. The reality, however, is that it's often challenging to always be firing on all cylinders at once. But by dedicating attention and resources to each, organizations can build a solid bedrock for meaningful work and employee success.

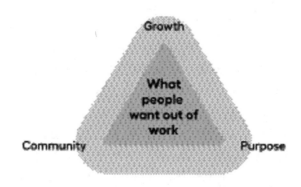

FIGURE 1.1

Purpose

Purpose is simple. It's what gives meaning to our lives. It's the reason we get out of bed every day. It's why we spend most of the waking hours of our adult lives working and doing what we do.

The way we find meaning in our careers is by seeing a clear connection between our personal purpose and how we spend our time at work. When we have that alignment, purpose becomes a way to understand the contributions we make to both our company and to society as a whole. It's this meaning that allows us to be fully engaged in, and dedicated to, the work we do day in and day out.

I try not to make a habit out of recommending self-help books, but if I have one to recommend, it's *How to Win Friends and Influence People* by Dale Carnegie (Pocket Books, 1998). One thing that Carnegie talks about early on in the book is that one of the most fundamental human desires is the need to feel important. This might sound selfish, and in some ways it is, but that doesn't mean it's a bad thing. It can be channeled to do something great, and it can be channeled into great work for a company that people believe helps the world and has impact.

There's not one "right" purpose; it's different for everyone. For some people, it may mean working for a company like charity: water (https://www.charitywater.org/) that has a social mission to build technology to help global communities get clean drinking water. For others, it may mean working for a company like Slack (https://slack.com/) which transformed communication at work for millions of people around the world.

Regardless of how you define success, knowing that your work matters to the world and that you have a chance to make a dent in the universe is so important to employees. And so, recognizing that, honoring that, and talking about it is very valuable when you're thinking about building your company.

In fact, I believe that the articulation of a company's purpose, and how it connects back to employees' purpose, is one of the most critical aspects of a leader's role. This may seem like a no-brainer, but it's not always easy. First, landing on your company's purpose – identifying why we exist and why we should continue to exist – can be a contentious and grueling exercise.

At Lattice, it took a lot of time and a lot of work to cultivate that answer. To first identify it and then sew it into the fabric of the company required serious reflection. What was our mission? Who was our product for? What kind of dent did we want to make in the world? And then there's the challenge of rallying the company around it on an ongoing basis, continually reminding and reinforcing the message.

Oftentimes, you have to make a choice between talking about the operational aspects of the business and talking about the *inspirational* aspects. Too often, leaders lean to the former, and don't give enough airtime to the latter. But when leaders are able to establish and keep that connection, they find that employees use it as fuel. Their enthusiasm serves as a self-perpetuating meaning machine: they share stories, speak passionately about what the company stands for, share personal lessons, and yes, put more discretionary effort toward achieving operational goals.

Community

Then there's *community*, which consists of the small groups, teams, or even the entire organization in which employees find trust, strong communication, respect, equality, and cooperation. Thriving internal communities amplify collective efforts to be made into something bigger and better than any individual employee could create on their own. Companies famous for their culture, like Apple, Google, and Nike, have created an entire ethos beyond merely selling products. Employees stand for a common goal or mission in which each member of the group is willing to contribute toward progress, and through this shared purpose and identity, strong relationships are formed. Community and purpose, in this way, go hand in hand, feeding into one another and bringing employees closer together.

I'll never forget the moment I realized that such a community had developed at Lattice. It was in the early days, and we had just moved the company from its previous home – in the one-bedroom apartment we were renting – to an actual office. I was walking down the stairs one day – from the second floor to the first, where most of our team worked – and I realized that I had a full view of the floor. People were huddled up behind computer screens. Some were sitting together, eating food and laughing. Others were headed out for a walk to get a coffee. It hit me: *These people like each other. They're having fun together. These folks are friends.*

It was a powerful moment. I had moved to San Francisco when I was 23. It was a new city for me, and the first friends that I made were through my job. My work was also my community. My coworkers – my fellow team members – were my people. The realization that we had built a place where other people were now forging those same kinds of connections, where this community was being fostered, nearly brought me to tears. After all, I knew how much being part of a community had meant to me.

This sense of community is a beautiful thing. It creates a sense of belonging that can motivate members to elevate their performance and dedication to what they care about most. Isolation, by contrast, creates hopelessness. We can't impact the complexities of the world and face up to major issues – like the coronavirus crisis or the movement for social and racial justice – without the support of others.

Community is very important to employees today, and there are a couple of reasons why. One potential reason is because work relationships have become stronger as companies have taken a more important role in employees' lives as more "traditional" communities like church or neighborhood have perhaps become less important. Another possible explanation is that the rise of the Internet and technology has led to a more globalized world. And as a result, the city, the nation, and the neighborhood have become less important constructs for people. You could even point to the decline of religion in major cities where this third community outside work and home has become less deep in our lives and, as a result, employees are seeking that more at work.

Whatever the reason, employees today have a deep hunger for community in their workplace. They want to be part of something. Community is a basic human need, and the workplace, more than ever, serves that. As such, it's important to know as people leaders that embracing challenge is not just OK, it's actually critical. Community, in many ways, is forged in the hardest of times. One that comes to mind for me is that I remember early on at Lattice, during the first six months, we were really struggling, and we just couldn't get our product to work and customers weren't taking to it. We'd been going for months, and my cofounder Eric and I were lying on the grass somewhere and we were just so *done*. We said, "Should we give up? It's so difficult." And we committed to each other that we were going to keep going for the other one. And that was the beginning of community. That was the first thing that we had at Lattice.

Another hard time was in 2017. I personally had a very tough period where my wife had a miscarriage, and I also had a parent pass away unexpectedly. It was one of the most difficult times of my life. But the company just embraced me and made me feel so supported, and I knew that we would all do that for each other. This inspired me and made me think, "Man, I will fight for this company. If I didn't have this, I don't know what would be happening."

Those are the moments that build community. Those are the trusting moments where you get through something hard together. And so, when you think about community at your companies and what employees need, it is not just about the celebrations and the parties and the cupcakes. Although those are great, and you should do them. But a lot of it is about those difficult moments where you commit to each other and you reaffirm your commitment to be a community together. That's what employees are seeking.

Growth

This sense of purpose and community can also help foster *growth*. Helping employees shape the future direction of their careers is rarely a focus in many organizations. Too often, companies are hyper-focused on the here and now, devoting the bulk of their attention to day-to-day operations at the expense of the bigger picture. While this meets short-term initiatives, it leaves them poorly equipped for success in the long run. The trouble is, many managers often find themselves too pressed for time to consider each employee's goals, strengths, areas for improvement, and the like, or simply don't know where to start. Areas of focus and development are deeply personal to each employee and cannot follow cookie-cutter guidelines. It's critical for employees and managers to be able to work together to build clear, personalized career development plans, so that each individual has a clear picture of what their path forward could look like.

But it's not just individual growth that's necessary, it's organizational growth, too. Not long after I founded Lattice, I did a series of interviews with various business and thought leaders, asking questions about the keys to building a good company culture. When I posed that question to Katelin Holloway, vice president of people and culture at Reddit, she told me that a winning, thriving company was most important.

This answer initially surprised me. "Isn't it deeper than that?" I thought. But, as Holloway explained to me, it's an environment of growth that allows for all the other things that make a culture strong. Growth provides fertile ground for employees to take on new responsibilities, new roles, and new problems.

That really stuck with me. An environment where people can't help but grow – that leads to great cultures.

Of course, growth can mean a lot of different things, as we learned during the pandemic. As COVID-19 gripped America and the world, Lattice's growth slowed, just as it did at many companies. We weren't promoting as many managers. Employees may not have been taking on new roles at the same rate, or any of the other things that we associated with growth before the pandemic. But also, as a company and as individuals, we have built some new muscles. We've learned things about ourselves. We've learned how to respond to challenges. We've learned how to do more with less.

That's growth, too.

Growth is the pursuit of improvement and progress that's core to the human experience. *Purpose* is knowing that what you're working on matters – that you're making that dent in the universe and that the work you do is felt and improves the lives of other people. And *community* is that sense of belonging and that fundamental need to be part of a group working toward that same purpose and progress. The combination of all of these things is what people really want out of work.

Culture is the vehicle we use to deliver these pillars of a successful, meaningful business. Companies with strong company cultures face the same challenges as companies that don't. But building these three things into your company culture will make it so much easier to navigate those challenges, and to give your employees the motivation and inspiration to work through them.

This has never been clearer than during the coronavirus pandemic. The defining characteristic of the business climate in 2020 was uncertainty. How can a business leader make hard decisions when it's unclear what the next three months – let alone the next year – will look like? Do you shift entirely to remote work?

Are you going to have to lay off employees or enact furloughs? These decisions are never easy to make, but that's especially so when the future is so hazy. That's where your company values kick in. They are your rock – a stabilizing force that provides at least some sense of clarity where there is little to be found.

HR teams likely already know this at some level. But for CEOs, the value of a strong culture is not always immediately apparent. Having happy employees is important, yes – but is it as crucial as organizational efficiency to a healthy bottom line? But having a strong culture isn't just about ensuring that those who work at your company are fulfilled and enjoying a sense of purpose and community and personal growth. Prioritizing culture and values is a critical strategic boon to any business, making an organization more efficient and nimble. When I had that bird's eye view over the office and saw the community that had developed at my company, I saw too that it was now bigger than me. There are some founders who might be troubled by that realization. It can be scary to realize that a company you worked so hard to build is capable of evolving on its own, without your fingerprints on every aspect of the organization. But for me, finding that Lattice didn't need me constantly to be breathing life into it in order to survive was freeing: there was so much it allowed me to focus on instead. Without a strong culture, executive teams tend to spend much more time working on repairs. A good culture, by contrast, is self-healing, taking care of itself organically. Likewise, companies with unhealthy organizational cultures tend to get bogged down by politics, internal bickering, or any number of other distractions. On the other hand, companies with a robust culture in place tend to be free of these toxic inefficiencies, making it easier to adapt and move forward.

That capability has always separated successful companies from less successful ones. But now, in a time when the business world is on the cusp of significant change thanks to the pandemic and other headwinds, the ability to evolve is more vital than ever. Of course, even having a culture that unites employees in common purpose, fosters a sense of community, and encourages growth won't make an organization immune from the challenges wrought by the pandemic or any other new challenges that may come our way. Further, the pillars might not all be firing on all cylinders at the same time. A company might endure a difficult time for growth – during the pandemic, for instance – by binding even closer together as a community, committing ourselves even more to our shared purpose. A good culture may be dynamic, but that dynamic, adaptive quality can get you through hard times.

In the chapters ahead, we'll look at the foundational elements needed of a People Strategy that addresses these needs of purpose, community, and growth, while also addressing the needs of the business to be successful and also being a place people want to work. Only through a smart People Strategy that puts employees first can companies better position themselves to absorb those blows, overcome obstacles, and adapt for future success.

Key Points

- Employees want their work to be about more than a paycheck. Companies that articulate a clear purpose ensure that employees find meaning in what they do.
- Community is more important to employees than ever. Fostering a sense of belonging can motivate team members to elevate their performance and dedication to the company's mission.

- Helping employees shape the future direction of their careers isn't always a focus in many organizations. But investing in employee development doesn't just mean that employees are likely to stick around for longer; it also compounds their ability to contribute to your organization in increasingly complex and creative ways.

CHAPTER

2

Hiring for Culture and Performance

The first step to building a successful People Strategy is, well, finding the right people. People are a company's most important asset. If a company cannot attract, grow, and retain talent, it's in trouble. But how do you find the right people? It's not just a matter of finding the most talented employees; it's about finding talented employees who share in the company's mission and can add to its culture.

Phrases like "culture fit" get thrown around a lot, but they can be notoriously difficult to define. Worse, they can sometimes be used to mask homogeneous and even discriminatory hiring practices. But when I think about the culture of an organization, I'm thinking about the personality of a company. I see fit as a two-way street, where a company and a person can see a great collaborative working relationship with shared goals and values. A good company culture is one in which lots of different personalities can gel within it. The key is finding people who can work well together, inspire each other, and share passions.

Bringing this kind of talent together is the foundation of a strong organizational culture. But while some of that culture forms organically, fostering a culture in which all employees are aligned and working toward a shared mission requires *intentionality* – particularly in our current landscape, with many companies navigating uncertainty and more employees working remotely. It requires the establishment of clear, authentic, and actionable company values.

It All Starts with Your Values. So, What Are They?

We had gone to Mexico, to the small town of Troncones, for our second annual company-wide off-site. The idea was simple: give everyone a long weekend to swim in the ocean, enjoy meals together, read by the pool, and get to know their Lattice coworkers in a new setting. But we did have one activity planned: an exercise to help us define our company values.

What a company values – and how it expresses those values – has never been more important. When competition for top talent is high, the bedrock principles that undergird an organization can help it differentiate itself. In a tumultuous business landscape, they can serve as a blueprint for navigating difficult times and can create a shared sense of purpose. Values can serve as a beacon for prospective employees, attracting those who are likeminded and share in the company's ethos; they can also serve the dual purpose of helping retain the talent they already have. Company values act like a behavioral north star, of sorts, which everyone from executives to the recent graduate starting their first job can look to in the day-to-day grind. But determining and expressing those values can prove difficult, as we would soon learn during that long weekend in Mexico.

We gathered in a big circle on the beach, underneath a tent. It was a postcard-perfect day – the waves lapping on the shore and the birds calling in the distance. Against this relaxing backdrop, one of our product designers handed out pens and three slips of paper to all 30 of the team members on the trip. He asked everyone to write down the qualities they most valued in their coworkers and themselves. After five minutes, we went around the circle, and employees would share one of their values with the group.

We continued like this for more than an hour. Maybe it was the serene setting, maybe it was the exercise itself, but I couldn't believe how much everyone opened up. One engineer, who normally was a quiet and reserved person, stood up and shared how determination and perseverance defined his approach to life. Several employees spoke about the importance of being honest, not just with others, but with ourselves. A marketer gave an impassioned speech about why creativity and independent thinking inspired him most. People laughed. People cried. People heard things from their coworkers they'd never known before. It felt like a major breakthrough.

At least that's what it felt like until we got back to the office.

When we took the notes we'd compiled during the exercise and distilled them to a few key values, they were cringingly bland. Empathy. Effort. Growth. Customer-obsession. Though the process was great, the result was a set of values that could have applied to any company. What organization doesn't value effort? Are there really companies that don't want to grow? Surely some companies don't put their customers first – but they probably don't stay in business for long.

I shared with the team the uninspiring values we'd arrived at, but I could tell it didn't stick. Everyone nodded along, then went on with their lives, and the values we had defined there on the beach that gorgeous day receded to the backs of their minds. Every so often, someone might invoke one of the values in a conversation – but even then, they seemed interchangeable. "Integrity is one of our values, right?" someone would ask. (It was not.) When employees remembered what the values were, they often found it difficult to apply them. How, exactly, does a content marketer or a product designer practice "empathy" in their daily work?

What we didn't realize at the time, but have learned since, is that there are "values" that point to the real thing (what you talk about in all-hands meetings and looks nice in posters on the company walls) and then there are *values*, which are the true qualities and actions that you deeply care about. In setting our original course, we established too much of the former and not enough of the latter. In other words, we tried to incorporate *everything*. But in defining our values too broadly, we failed to define our values at all. The set of principles we'd outlined were so bland that they failed to resonate even with those of us who'd established them.

It's hard to admit to yourself that you failed. But we knew we'd missed the mark. Six months after announcing our new company values, we decided to try again. How could we take the things we knew we valued as a group and articulate them in a way that would *mean* something? How could we define our values in a way that was memorable, unique to Lattice, and not only described, but inspired the feelings and ideas that we wanted to promote?

We started by asking ourselves which phrases we used organically on that day in Troncones, looking to find something in the words we used that might embody the things we care about. One of those phrases was "Ship, Shipmate, Self." At the time, we'd been using the mantra quite a bit – when decisions arose that threw the company, teammates, and individuals into conflict. It was a reminder to put the company's well-being and success over that of the individual and to put the well-being and success of our colleagues over our own.

It was memorable. It was real. Most importantly, it was a tangible reminder that employees could use to guide their decision making in any circumstance.

We had our first value.

Next, we referred to a phrase that we'd been using around the office about the virtue of doing real work and of focusing on inputs over outputs: "Chop Wood, Carry Water." We had borrowed the mantra from the title of Joshua Medcalf's book, *Chop Wood Carry Water: How to Fall in Love with the Process of Becoming Great* (CreateSpace, 2015), an insightful exploration of – among other things – the importance of embracing the process rather than merely the result. In this story of a boy training to become a samurai warrior, our hero learns early on the wisdom of paying attention to the action at hand:

Akira gathered the newly arrived apprentices and informed them of their first task: for the rest of the morning, they would chop wood and carry water.

John was surprised and confused. He addressed his teacher with the proper title of respect that they had been taught: "Akira-sensei, what do you mean?"

The old man explained that their community was outfitted with every modern convenience, except for heat and running water. Instead of using gas or electricity, they burned wood for heat when the weather grew cold. And in order to use water in the bathrooms and kitchen, it had to be brought by hand from a well outside. Thus, in order for the community to use water and stay warm during the winter, the community depended on everyone to chop wood and carry water.

"But when will we get to shoot?" John wondered aloud.

Akira just smiled. "Shooting will come soon enough. But first, you must chop wood, and carry water."

John was frustrated, but he obeyed. He trusted his sensei's wisdom, and knew that in time, they would move on to more exciting things.[1]

At Lattice, we had taken the lesson of the parable to heart in our daily work: it connected with our product, our pursuit for constant improvement, and our belief that focusing on the process will lead to good results. We made it our second value.

By now, we were rolling.

Reflecting on those things we wanted to capture in our values, we decided that we needed somehow to allude to the importance of pragmatism, transparency, ambition, and growth. "Clear Eyes" became our next guiding principle, alluding to our goal of approaching our work, colleagues, customers, and ourselves with clarity and honesty. We believe that starting from a place of truth will make us successful and happy in the long run. We harness pragmatism as a superpower. After some debate, we arrived next at our last principle: "What's Next?" (See Figure 2.1.) The question served as a reminder to always be looking forward.

FIGURE 2.1

---

[1]Joshua Medcalf, *Chop Wood Carry Water: How to Fall in Love with the Process of Becoming Great* (CreateSpace Independent Publishing Platform, 2015), p. 7.

At Lattice, we have an insatiable appetite to grow, to improve, and to look for the next horizon. Whenever we arrive at a destination, we see it as the beginning of a new journey. Our work will never be done.

A great deal changed for us once we managed to zero in on our company values. Where previously we were operating under the auspices of high-minded but not especially meaningful or memorable buzzwords, we now had a clear guiding light to give us direction. We integrated those four values into every fiber of our organization, and in doing so we were able to distribute the decision-making process across the company. Even without founders or managers present, everyone at the company knew how to operate – how to run meetings, how to hire, how to hold a performance review. Our company values serve as a road map for how to behave, even when those who set out those values aren't in the room.

Defining your company values can be challenging, but it is undoubtedly worth it. Consider Airbnb, one of the most successful start-ups in recent memory. A company culture grounded in well-defined values alone isn't enough to ensure success, but CEO Brian Chesky has attributed a great deal of his company's success to its commitment to a core philosophy – one unique to his organization. "Integrity, honesty – those aren't core values," Chesky said in a 2014 speech at Stanford University. "Those are values that everyone should have. But there have to be like three, five, six things that are unique to you. And you can probably think about this in your life. What is different about you, than every single other person, if you could only tell them three or four things, you would want them to know about you."

Values have the power to shape both the employee experience as well as your brand. Those values not only help give your company identity and direction, they also bind employees to one another in service of a common goal. Once defined, values should

help guide your decision-making process, both at the management level and in the day-to-day trenches for all employees. For
the values to work, they must be specific to your company. And
they need to be bold.

For example, "effort" is not a good company value because
it's hard to imagine any company that doesn't prize hard work.
For a value to resonate, the opposite must be able to be equally
true; it would be reasonable, for instance, for a company to
encourage employees to put themselves and their own growth
and needs ahead of those of their coworkers and the company
itself. That's just not how we envision things at Lattice. Discov-
ering, articulating, and reinforcing those values that are unique
to you will serve as a compass for both management and individual contributor employees.

Make sure that your values are both meaningful and authentic; phrases, more than just individual words, can better articulate
a company principle. While a word may point to a concept, it can
feel hollow or unspecific or difficult to apply. Furthermore, it's
important to have a description that not only defines the value,
but can also clearly articulate how it applies specifically to your
organization. We all may value "honesty" in the abstract; but
when the rubber meets the road, it may look a little different
from one person or from one company to the next. Put differently: it's not only what your company values – it's how your
company values it. Don't just pay lip service toward values. Make
them honest and real and strive to live up to them every day. As
John Moss, managing director of home-decor company English
Blinds, once put it: "Values are better felt than formulated."

I love the way Nathalie McGrath of The People Design
House describes the importance of values in building and defining culture in a post she wrote on Medium:

> Culture is not one thing, but instead an end product, it's the result
> of actions, behaviors, and decisions made as a group of people.

The real driver of culture is what people do and say. Behaviors and decision making can be complicated and are influenced by various things such as: where an individual grew up, went to school, and where they last worked. The simplified version is that behaviors and decisions are based upon a set of beliefs and values.

Culture is the result of behaviors & decisions. Behaviors & decisions are based upon your beliefs and values. Beliefs are the conscious or unconscious assumptions you have about the world and how it works. Values are what you deem important about those beliefs.[2]

When companies fail to establish clear, authentic, and meaningful values, they're missing out on more than a well-defined mission. Companies with confusing or hollow values often lack a strong culture. McGrath went on to say in her piece, "A culture breathes the life that the founders put into [a company] from the beginning – their values and beliefs shape the behaviors and decisions that help the company flourish or fail."

At Lattice, we look at "culture" as the personality of an organization, the way its various moving parts interact, and how it applies its abstract mission in real life. But very often there's a disconnect between how a company's leaders envision their culture and how the employees experience it day in and day out.

This is surprisingly common in the United States. According to a 2016 Gallup poll, just 27 percent of people surveyed strongly believed in their company's values; even fewer, 23 percent, felt confident that they could apply those values to their daily work. The result, the researchers found, was a pattern of "inconsistency and confusion for employees and customers" across several different organizations and industry sectors. "Culture can be a formidable driver of performance," the researchers wrote.

---

[2]Nathalie McGrath, "The Building Blocks of Culture," Medium.com (Jan 16, 2020), https://medium.com/@NathalieMcGrath/the-building-blocks-of-culture-3f3659187b95

"But when a company struggles with gaps between the desired culture and the actual culture, this hinders it from achieving performance goals and meeting customers' needs."[3]

If values help foster a strong identity, mission, and clarity of purpose, a lack of values leaves a company without clear direction and common goals. That's never a good position for any organization, but it may be especially so when it comes to millennial and Gen Z employees, who tend to be extremely ambitious, growth hungry, and eager for a sense of community that aligns with their own principles.

So, what do you do after you establish your company values?

It certainly doesn't end on a beach in Mexico – it's something you have to reinforce consistently, including in the hiring process.

Three Tips for Writing Company Values That Inspire

Every great company needs a culture code – but when it comes time to formalize yours, don't be surprised if you get writer's block. Values have the power to shape the employee experience and your employer brand. Don't skimp on the process.

1. Make Employees Part of the Process

If you want buy-in from employees, you need to make them part of the process. But that doesn't necessarily mean putting everyone on a beach, as we did at Lattice. In some cases,

---

[3] Nate Dvorak and Bailey Nelson, "Few Employees Believe in Their Company's Values," *Gallup Business Journal* (Sept 13, 2016), https://news.gallup.com/businessjournal /195491/few-employees-believe-company-values.aspx

you'll actually want to identify a committee – whether it's top performers or through an employee survey – who you feel exemplify the values you know are already there at your company but have yet to be defined. Your final committee should bring perspectives from across company locations; departments; management levels; and, of course, race, gender, national origin, and sexual orientation groups.

2. Be Original – but Stay Authentic

Communication, respect, and integrity – these are three core values you would have seen on display at Enron headquarters in 2001. Chances are that you've seen at least one of these used by a former employer.

While traditional values like these aren't problematic on their own, without more context, they can seem hollow or open to misinterpretation. In lieu of single words, consider phrases, and make sure to include a few descriptive lines to orient those who are new to them.

Over 20 companies shared their values with us. Many were especially unique and painted a vivid picture of their respective company cultures. Following are some of the highlights:

- Make Our Clients Heroes
- Thick as Thieves
- Work Smart to Live Well
- Attitude Is Everything
- Produce and Protect
- Elevate Others
- Leave the World a Better Place

- Develop Daily
- Break Our Own Glass Ceilings
- Empathy and Endeavor

3. Don't Be Afraid to Iterate and Make Changes

Choosing core values is a high-stakes decision. But companies and priorities evolve – and when things no longer feel like a fit, it's okay to go back to the drawing board. While new values might become necessary because of a merger, acquisition, or pivot in the business, sometimes leaders "just know" when it's time to make a clean break.

When It's Time to Hire, Hire *for* Your Values

Daniel Chait, cofounder and CEO of the recruiting platform Greenhouse (https://www.greenhouse.io/) and a thought leader on the changing world of work, likes to talk about the importance of reinforcing company values. If a company only pays lip service to its principles, he told me once, interviewers will not make them a priority when they talk to job candidates. "If they know the person is going to show up and not really get evaluated on the values, and that it's really just about their coding or their sales, then they're going to kind of fake it through the interview process," Chait said. To ensure that those values are fully integrated into the hiring process, those who are most representative of them should be involved in the hiring process, from designing the job description to interviewing. "The whole process should be influenced by the people who best represent the values you hold," Chait said.

Employers should use company values to find not just *good* employees, but employees who are a *good fit* for the company – for its culture and mission. The values that a company projects are akin to the Bat Signal, drawing in prospective employees not just looking for a paycheck, but to help the company realize its vision.

Include company values in job descriptions for open roles to entice applicants who both align with the company's culture *and* who can add to it. In any hiring climate, but especially one in which competition for talent is high, it can be challenging to bring in and retain the best employees when hiring managers struggle to articulate company values to prospective employees. This makes it more important than ever to differentiate based on values and mission. After all, even the most talented individuals can be misplaced or fail to realize their full potential if the values are misaligned. Building job descriptions around company values can help define both the job *and* the type of applicant you are seeking. For example, take this job listing for a Product Designer position we had open at Lattice:

Product Designer – Lattice

About Lattice

Lattice is on a mission to build cultures where employees and their companies thrive. In an age where innovation is happening all around us, there's commonality – people are driving these changes. We offer a solution that helps companies put employees first. Lattice is a people management tool that offers performance reviews, employee engagement surveys, real-time feedback, weekly check-ins, and goal setting in a way that allows companies to focus on employee development, growth, and engagement. Since launching in 2016, we have grown to over 1,300 customers globally, including brands like Slack, WeWork, Reddit, Glossier, and Asana.

We're a small and impactful team of product engineers continuously working to improve our product and our craft. We use a modern, cutting-edge tech stack and love experimenting with new technologies to create our products. We are really excited to find a person that has the experience and ability to own our infrastructure and improve our development experience.

About the Role

You're a Product Designer and you're sure of your process. You have been at it for 3+ years and enjoy sharing your knowledge with your fellow teammates. Research isn't just a buzzword to you, it's a constant state of learning about your customers. You over-invest in the visual and interaction portion of your work and consider yourself a craftsperson. Everything is your problem. You care about why you're building something, not just what you're building. You consider the technical, product, and business needs of the company with each decision. You're based in San Francisco or are willing to relocate, and you are eligible to work in the United States.

Responsibilities

Because our team is small, you'll be given lots of responsibility and opportunities to impact the overall product and business. You'll work with the team to build product-defining features as well as be a decision maker in what direction we take the product.

- You'll collaborate with Product, Engineering, and Customer Success to help identify the needs of our customers, prioritize our efforts, tirelessly iterate, and ship world-class solutions.

- You'll socialize the design process to non-product functions.
- You'll embody our principles.
- You'll push our visual and interaction execution further.

Nice to Have

- Strong portfolio of high-quality visual and interaction design execution
- Prior experience designing for desktop platforms and data visualization
- Prior experience in People Management software or SaaS companies
- Comfortable working independently and elevating design thinking
- Ability to work within our established frameworks and contribute to them
- Previous experience working on design teams

Why Lattice?

- We invest in the personal and professional growth of every employee because we believe growth leads to both business impact and personal fulfillment
- The opportunity to join an experienced and ambitious team that is passionate about solving customers' needs and loves coming to work every day
- Partner with 1,500+ companies around the world to make sure their employees are engaged and performing at a high level

- A culture that encourages and promotes professional growth and development, with continuous learning reimbursements
- Competitive salary, equity, and benefits
- Centrally located Financial District office in San Francisco and New York
- Flexible vacation/time-off policy

Implicit in this job description are our values. Phrases like *everything is your problem* and *you care about why you're building something, not just what you're building* allude to our values of personal responsibility (Ship, Shipmate, Self) and focusing on the process over the outcome (Chop Wood, Carry Water). Simply having the right skills is not enough on its own to ensure success in a role; the person you hire must be the right fit for the company. The interview process is an opportunity to determine if a prospective employee matches the values outlined in the job description and, therefore, will make a good addition to the team. Interviewing a potential new hire is something of an art. The goal is to elicit openness from the job candidate, which can be difficult – both for the interviewer and the interviewee. After all, it's not a setting that lends itself naturally to openness. It can be nerve-wracking for all parties involved. Both the employer and the prospective employee want to make a good impression. And each is trying to figure out the other, attempting to gauge if this is where the applicant belongs.

The key is to ask open-ended questions. Just as the job description above nods at our company values without explicitly stating them, the questions we ask in an interview are crafted to assess fit without tacitly coaching the employee to tell us what we want to hear. Rather than running down the list of your company values and asking the potential hire to give examples of each, ask broader questions of the interviewee, getting the applicant to demonstrate their values rather than list them as part of a stock answer to a stock question like, "So, what are your values?" For example, if one of your values is "Ownership," ask candidates for an example of a time when they took the fall when a project went awry. To hammer this home with the interviewers within your company, consider incorporating values into your interview scorecards as well.

The goal is to determine both if the prospective hire's values align with those of the company and if they will also bring something unique to the company's culture. Indeed, a good "culture fit" not only reflects the company culture, but also how the new hire adds to it. "[We're] hopefully evolving and improving with every new hiring class," Box CEO and cofounder Aaron Levie told me once. "You want to be learning from new employees as well as more tenured ones." It's incredibly powerful when the right person gets into the right role – when a person is both meeting the company's needs and the company is meeting theirs, so there is a perfect symbiosis between the two.

Of course, company culture is not a static thing. Companies, like people, evolve and change over time. Sometimes, that change can be a consequence of larger forces – the way, for instance, that the COVID-19 pandemic forced many companies and their employees to adapt to remote work and changed the way workers communicate, collaborate, and connect. But these changes do not always take place on such a large scale.

Early on at Lattice, we had an extremely talented salesperson. He was a major contributor, liked by everyone at the company, and understood our business inside and out. He was easily one of our best hires. But after a great year or so, things began to change. Our business was growing up, and the needs of each job were changing dramatically. He seemed to lose interest, and as time went on, the enthusiasm and energy that made him so successful began to dry up. Rather than adapting to the new needs of our business, he remained in the old mold and was unable – or unwilling – to adapt. As his performance declined, he started looking out for himself at the expense of his teammates and the business. In short, he was not chopping wood and carrying water, not putting his ship and shipmates ahead of himself, and not looking ahead to what's next. Fortunately, he did have clear eyes. He recognized that his values and the company no longer aligned, and we parted ways amicably.

Now, was this person a bad hire, just because he left the company? Of course not. A fit can change over time. Maybe a company's values evolve. Maybe an employee's values do. Either way, such evolution is something that companies should embrace. For example, I remember leaving Teespring with the vision of starting something that was a better fit for me and knowing that the best ideas spark when we push ourselves toward an idea that fits us better. We wanted to give the same opportunities to our employees at Lattice, and that's why at Lattice we created the Invest in Your People Fund, setting aside money to invest in our employees who go on to start their own companies.

The employee-job fit is vital to satisfaction and productivity; without it, an employee most often isn't motivated to bring their whole self to work. Similarly, the employer-employee relationship isn't just about satisfying the needs of the company; it's also about meeting the professional needs of the employee. Unfortunately for both employees and companies, work has too often been seen as an arduous and unpleasant reality of life – something we trudge our way through to get from one weekend to the next. But work doesn't have to be a drag.

It could be our *ikigai*; that is, our reason for getting out of bed in the morning. This Japanese concept sits at the axis of four elements: a person's passion, their skill set, a need in the

FIGURE 2.2

world, and compensation (see Figure 2.2). An ideal employee-employer fit will provide that *ikigai*. I always hope that Lattice can fulfill that fit for our employees, but sometimes we just don't – and that's okay. When that's the case, we want to be there to support them emotionally, tactically, and financially.

My biggest goal, personally and for Lattice, has always been to make work meaningful. People are a company's most important asset, and the goal is to get great people into your organization, set them up to be as successful as they can be, and keep them happy. Contrary to what some companies seem to believe, you don't need a ping-pong table in the office to foster a great work culture, or even to go off-site to Mexico; a great work culture is simply about putting people first, establishing and living up to your company values, and finding and nurturing talent that fits those values. In short, it's about treating your employees like they're the most important resource your company has.

After all, they are.

Key Points

- Values are an aspirational code that companies build their culture around.

- Values have the power to shape the employee experience and your employer brand.

- Companies should use their values in the hiring process, not to identify candidates who would "fit" into the culture, but to identify those who would enrich it.

3

Performance and the Importance of Feedback

I am profoundly unathletic, and sports analogies don't come naturally to me. But indulge me while I try, in hopes of communicating the importance of continuous feedback.

Imagine you are a baseball coach. Your pitcher is struggling with his control – his fastball is up, his slider is down, and his curve is hanging over the middle of the plate. Seemingly unable to get anyone out, the other team's batters are teeing off on him with each at bat. As he grows increasingly frustrated, you pay close attention to his form, attempting to diagnose the problem. Soon enough, you've got it figured out – a small, but crucial aspect of his delivery is off. With one minor adjustment, you're fairly certain he'd find his groove. One tweak and your pitcher would be unhittable.

What would you do? Would you head out to the mound and give him a quick tip then and there so that he could make an immediate adjustment? Or would you wait six months, allowing the minor issue not to only derail the possibility of winning *this* game, but also set him – and the team – off course for the rest of the season?

Even if you've never been in a dugout before, you know exactly what you would do – you'd have the pitcher fix the issue when it first arises. It's common sense.

And yet, so many companies have a performance feedback culture that features exactly the opposite; they wait until the end of year. For decades, the dreaded "performance review" was a once-a-year source of anxiety for employees, who went into their annual evaluation not knowing if they were about to be promoted or fired.

Even though the gold standard for performance management has evolved, many companies still operate the old way. These performance review meetings often feel unnatural and strained, and, in most cases, aren't particularly effective. According to a recent Gallup survey, just 14 percent of employees strongly agreed that their annual review inspires them to improve their performance.

And why should they? Traditional performance reviews have been so bound up in pay, position, and punishment, making it easy to lose sight of their actual purpose; that is, ensuring that employees are performing to their fullest potential, being recognized for the good work they're doing, and being positioned and equipped for success. The old model – with its rigid formality, its unproductive sense of high stakes, and its infrequent timetable – is simply not an effective appraisal mechanism. In fact, not only does the traditional performance model fail to improve employee performance, but according to one study, "Is It Time to Put the Performance Review on a PIP?" by Dori Meinert in April 2015, it actually results in *worse* performance more than a third of the time![1]

Why has the traditional performance review proved so counterproductive?

The reasons are numerous.

What we have come to think of as the old standard of performance reviews may have its roots in the Industrial Revolution, with the era's narrow and often ugly preoccupation with productivity. As *Fast Company* noted in 2018, by World War I and World War II, the United States military was using metrics to "identify and dismiss poor performers and then to rank enlisted soldiers based on their potential to ascend to leadership."[2] Soon, this concept migrated from the military to the business world, and by the middle of the twentieth century, such performance evaluations had become central to employee management, linked to raises, job titles, promotions, and termination decisions. By the 1980s, General Electric CEO Jack Welch had popularized his famous – or perhaps infamous – "rank and yank" system, in which employees were ranked according to performance, and the bottom 10 percent was "yanked" from the company. While the company finally phased that system out more than a decade ago, the archaic concept continues to live on throughout the business world. "We've been conditioned by 20th-century corporate culture to accept [traditional performance reviews] as the norm," as Delphi Group Founder Thomas Koulopoulos once put it in

---

[1]Dori Meinert, "Is It Time to Put the Performance Review on a PIP?," *HR Magazine* (April 2015), https://www.shrm.org/hr-today/news/hr-magazine/Pages/0415-qualitative -performance-reviews.aspx

[2]Lydia Dishman, "The Complicated and Troubled History of the Annual Performance Review," *Fast Company* (Nov 7, 2018), https://www.fastcompany.com/90260641/the -complicated-and-troubled-history-of-the-annual-performance-review

his article "Performance Reviews Are Dead. Here's What You Should Do Instead" in *Inc.* magazine.[3]

This system has proven to be deeply unhelpful, both for employees and for companies. For employees, the review process is often full of anxiety and stress, almost akin to the standardized tests that many of us feared in school. And, like those exams, the reviews sometimes come loaded with high stakes for an employee's future. For companies, this method has proven to be ineffectual and time-consuming. According to one study by the Society for Human Resource Management, 95 percent of managers are dissatisfied with their performance appraisal process, and 90 percent don't even believe such reviews provide accurate information.

That would be troubling enough on its own, but when you add in the amount of resources the old-school system eats up, it is even more concerning. Per that same study, about two-thirds of employees surveyed said the review process ate into their productivity and didn't seem relevant to their day-to-day work anyway. Meanwhile, according to Gallup, traditional performance reviews can cost companies between $2.4 million and $35 million in lost hours per 10,000 employees. It's as if we're all paying an enormous tax, and instead of receiving value on the other side, it's being destroyed.

The old model of performance reviews wastes time and money with little to show for it other than stress and general awkwardness for all parties involved. So, perhaps not surprisingly, more and more companies in recent years have been rethinking their performance review and feedback processes.

Adobe is one notable example. In 2012, noticing spikes in retention problems right around performance review time, the

---

[3]Thomas Koulopoulos, "Performance Reviews Are Dead. Here's What You Should Do Instead," *Inc. Magazine* (Feb 25, 2018), https://www.inc.com/thomas-koulopoulos /performance-reviews-are-dead-heres-what-you-should-do-instead.html

company decided to change things up – shifting away from the old model of formal annual reviews to more casual and consistent check-ins between employees and their managers. The new system got results, allowing the organization to take a more team-oriented approach. "So many of the processes and functions in HR are practices that were adopted in a different era," Donna Morris, the company's senior vice president of global people and places, told *HR Magazine* in 2015. "I think we need to re-evaluate some of our core practices and processes."[4] Several companies – including GE, which popularized the hard-nosed "rank and yank" system to begin with – have begun doing just that.

At Lattice, we have been a leader of that shift, providing companies with the right tools and mindset to give healthier, more productive, and more effective employee feedback. How?

Continuous Feedback = No Surprises

It starts with a shift in thinking. Performance feedback needs to be ongoing and collaborative – stripped of the formality, the high stakes – and focused more on helping people grow than on evaluating them. Consistent check-ins and real-time feedback ensure that criticism – or praise, for that matter – does not come as a surprise to employees. Think about that struggling pitcher from the beginning of this chapter: it doesn't make sense to blindside him, months later, with the feedback that there was some imperfection in his wind-up. He should have been made aware of his performance, and given suggestions on how he could adapt, the moment the issue became apparent.

---

[4]Dori Meinert, "Is It Time to Put the Performance Review on a PIP?," *HR Magazine* (April 2015), https://www.shrm.org/hr-today/news/hr-magazine/Pages/0415-qualitative -performance-reviews.aspx

After all, little is gained by keeping employees in the dark about their performance until that one dreaded day a year. All of the time spent not addressing issues with their performance is time both the employee and the company have lost, allowing the sub-par work to continue longer when, oftentimes, a simple diagnosis could have allowed the employee in question to right the course. The tech investor Keith Rabois explained the following to me once:

> The best way to do it is to tie to whenever the object of the feedback is most relevant . . . So, when someone has a presentation, for example, or makes an argument about a certain initiative, it's better to tie that feedback to that specific problem because then you can help their brain adjust to, "Oh, I can see how I could have done this better or why it would matter," versus a generic statement three months later.[5]

Provide continuous feedback, as opposed to annual reviews, to ensure that your input is more effective, more actionable, and less surprising for employees (see Figure 3.1). In a good feedback culture, employees are guided through two-way conversations in which the communication flows both ways, and neither employees nor organizations are left feeling blindsided. Managers should always be giving employees constructive feedback, identifying when expectations are and aren't met, praising employees for successes, and keeping employees informed about ways they can improve. This constant feedback loop does not necessarily replace more formal check-ins and reviews. But it ensures that what is said at the review is never a surprise. In a good feedback culture, employees won't be surprised by what their managers tell them at performance reviews – because they'll have already heard it.

---

[5]Keith Rabois, "Keith Rabois on How to Find and Grow Talent," Lattice website (Oct 18, 2016), https://lattice.com/interview/keith-rabois-on-how-to-find-and-grow-talent

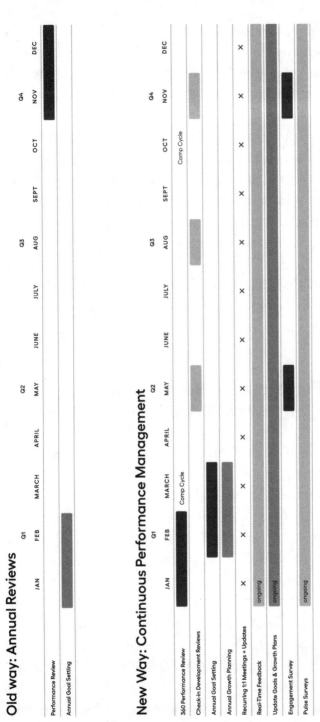

Old way: Annual Reviews

	Q1			Q2			Q3			Q4		
	JAN	FEB	MARCH	APRIL	MAY	JUNE	JULY	AUG	SEPT	OCT	NOV	DEC
Performance Review												
Annual Goal Setting												

New Way: Continuous Performance Management

	Q1			Q2			Q3			Q4		
	JAN	FEB	MARCH	APRIL	MAY	JUNE	JULY	AUG	SEPT	OCT	NOV	DEC
360 Performance Review			Comp Cycle							Comp Cycle		
Check-in Development Reviews												
Annual Goal Setting												
Annual Growth Planning												
Recurring 1:1 Meetings + Updates	X	X	X	X	X	X	X	X	X	X	X	X
Real-Time Feedback	ongoing											
Update Goals & Growth Plans	ongoing											
Engagement Survey												
Pulse Surveys	ongoing											

Performance Review: Fully 360 (self, peer, upward, downward) with scoring. Templates to be revamped to be lighter weight and better balance of qual/quant.

Quarterly Check-ins: Efficient self and downward reviews.

FIGURE 3.1

A good feedback culture doesn't only work from the top down, with managers communicating needs for adjustment and the like to those below them in the company hierarchy. In a modern work environment, employees are also deeply connected to their peers, team members, and coworkers. Communication should be ongoing and free-flowing, with open lines of communication, and employees should be made to feel comfortable that their coworkers will be able and willing to provide them with both positive and constructive feedback. Ideally, the employee will also feel confident in judging their own strengths and weaknesses, and safe to assess their own performance with clear eyes and without fear – something we certainly value at Lattice.

Clearly, a good feedback culture is important for the vitality of an organization. But how do you foster this kind of environment and maintain it, even in a changing world of work?

High Performance Begins with High Expectations: SMART Goals Versus OKRs

I like to think of feedback culture as a performance wellness system that involves continuous check-ins, adjustments, and bigger check-ups. It's not unlike a person's health: There are the things that we do every day to maintain our personal well-being, such as exercising, eating healthy, and perhaps taking vitamins. There are little adjustments that we make along the way – cutting down on certain foods we know aren't good for us, making a point to get more sleep, or perhaps taking up yoga. And then we head to our physician for our yearly check-up, where we get a more holistic and long-term view of our health. Maintaining a healthy feedback culture is similar. Continuous feedback, both from managers and coworkers, is the daily upkeep. One-on-ones further help us take stock of what we're doing well and what we need to adjust along the way. And the performance reviews, held quarterly or twice a year, are the bigger checkups to ensure that everything's working as it should and to set a plan for those things that might need attention.

Many companies use goals as the anchor for expectation-setting, feedback, and measuring performance. Goals make an excellent foundation since they make clear what success looks like. If the review process is meant to determine whether expectations are being met or exceeded, firmly establishing those benchmarks can be extremely valuable. That's why setting goals is the first step in the Lattice feedback process.

When we set personal goals, they tend to look a lot like New Year's resolutions: get more exercise, make more time for family, stick to a budget, and so on. But setting individual or company goals for performance includes some very specific needs to address:

1. Communicate what to focus on (and – maybe more importantly – what to block out)
2. Track progress and motivate employees
3. Help define and meet career development milestones
4. Show how different initiatives are connected to one another
5. Give employees direction while supporting their autonomy

Knowing how deeply important and foundational these goals will be, you don't want to just throw a few "resolutions" on the whiteboard at the start of the year, providing no guidance beyond that. That's where goal-making frameworks come in. I like two popular frameworks for corporate goal setting – SMART goals and OKRs.

SMART goals are commonly associated with Peter Drucker's "Management by Objectives" concepts. SMART goals encourage the goal setter (usually an employee or team leader) to detail how the intended goal will be accomplished, balancing expectations with reality. A SMART system follows this mnemonic formula for creating effective goals:

SPECIFIC: Does the goal have specific means and ends?

MEASURABLE: Can the goal be measured and how?

ACTIONABLE: Are there specific actions that can lead to this goal?

RELEVANT: Is this goal relevant to the work?

TIME-BOUND: What is the time frame? Is it a set deadline, or is it on a regular schedule?

Let's say that you have a non-SMART goal to "Close more business in Q1."

You can make this goal SMART by adding more detail: "Close (actionable) $1M (measurable) by the end of Q1 (time-bound) by bringing in qualified leads through cold calls and demos (specific and relevant)."

Companies, including Lattice, like to formalize goals one step further with another goal-setting framework called *OKRs* (*Objectives and Key Results*). OKRs were famously developed by Andy Grove at Intel and passed down to John Doerr, who brought them to Google. Today, thousands of organizations from Spotify to the United States Navy use OKRs as a key management tool.

Organizations implement OKRs as a way to align company, team, and individual goals to measurable results. They serve as a performance-management framework that allows organizations to ensure that everyone is moving in the same direction. This model encourages companies and employees to prioritize those objectives that will have the biggest impact on the company and its overall mission. Moreover, they make those goals transparent and serve as a measuring stick for the progress employees are making toward their stated objectives. This empowers members of an organization to do their best work, gauge the impact of their work, and stretch beyond what initially seemed possible so that companies can achieve extraordinary results.

Once you're sold on OKRs as a concept, it's important to learn to do them right.

The structure of the OKR is simple:

OBJECTIVE: Where do I want to go?
KEY RESULTS: How do I get there?

The *Objective* is the goal of the company, team, or employee. The *Key Results* are the concrete steps necessary to accomplish that goal. The beauty of the framework is that it can be repeated from the top of the organization down to the individual, which creates a tapestry of goals that keeps everyone aligned and moving in the same direction. The highest level of the company sets the organization's strategic goals. Those goals then trickle down the company hierarchy, informing team and individual objectives at every level of the organization. Establishing clear, measurable, and ambitious objectives in this way can be the difference between an efficient and dynamic organization and one that lacks direction and purpose. Organizational leaders get everyone on the same page, ensuring that everyone from the executive level to the lowest rung is working directionally toward the same objectives. This empowers employees, too, allowing them to understand more clearly how their work contributes to their company's overall objectives.

Objectives should be ambitious, with Key Results that are concrete and linked to measurable milestones. Objectives should be divided into performance goals, such as an employee raising their sales quota, and development goals, like improving their time management. Just make sure development goals are considered outside of the guise of operational goals.

In most cases, these goals should not be directly tied to compensation. Remember: this is not the traditional performance management model, where employees are made to fear reviews; this is about ensuring that employees are aligned with company strategy and contributing to their highest potential.

Getting Started with OKRs

When you're ready to take the OKR plunge, set a target to start your company's OKR process roughly six weeks before the beginning of a new fiscal year or quarter. This will give you enough time to prepare for effective annual and quarterly goals.

1. Identify high-level company objectives and key results.

The management team identifies the 3–5 core company objectives – either yearly or quarterly objectives. These objectives should originate from the company's high-level mission/vision, but they can range in focus from the bottom line (increase sales by 200 percent) to company values (only use renewable energy to operate the business). After deciding the objectives, the team should identify the measurable results needed to accomplish these objectives. For example, if the sales team wants to increase sales by 200 percent, then a key result might be hiring five account executives. These key results will help guide the objectives for the next tier of the organization (teams).

2. Decide on a system for organizing OKRs.

For companies of all sizes, tracking OKRs can be a challenging process. For example, Google built its own internal tools, while others use ad hoc methods like spreadsheets. A growing number of companies are using dedicated goal-tracking software tools like Lattice. These tools can be extremely helpful when it comes to company alignment and communication, especially when combined with other interlocking processes like performance review tracking or feedback delivery.

3. Collaborate with team leads to draft departmental objectives.

Set up a meeting with the heads of your different teams/departments to cover a few major topics:

OKR Overview: What are OKRs, and why are they important? Why does the management team want to use them?

OKR 101: How do OKRs work in practice? What's a good OKR and what's a bad OKR?

Company OKR Negotiation: Explain how the management team is thinking about the company OKRs, and how department leaders will collaborate on the final company list along with their team OKRs. At the end of this step, department heads should have a clear understanding of company OKRs and also have a draft for their respective departments.

4. Roll out OKRs to the entire company.

Now that you have your department leaders on board, it's time to present the OKRs to the entire company at an all-hands meeting. Make sure to provide context around why OKRs are important and how they will work at the company so that employees have proper expectations around how to interact with the OKR system.

5. Managers work with individual contributors to draft employee OKRs.

This level is where most of the OKR work will happen – Google says that roughly 60 percent of a company's overall OKRs come from the bottom up. After the all-hands meeting, managers will meet with team members to kick off that individual OKR writing process. This conversation is a negotiation – a two-way conversation where you start by outlining what an employee wants to work on versus what the manager wants the individual to work on. By having this collaborative conversation of reviewing and even resetting goals four times every year, individual contributors are empowered to make decisions about their career and day-to-day work.

6. Calibrate and present final OKRs company-wide.

After those individual conversations, it's important for team leads and management to take a step back and see how they might have changed any of the team or high-level company OKRs. After management feels good about the OKRs for the year/quarter, it's time to present the OKRs at a second company-wide meeting and finalize the direction for the coming year/quarter.

7. Monitor OKR progress.

Throughout the next quarter (and year), both managers and individual contributors should continually monitor the progression of individual OKRs to make sure that the company is moving toward the company goals.

Salesforce CEO Marc Benioff on Performance Management

The OKR model is only one performance management framework. Salesforce CEO Marc Benioff established the V2MOM (Vision, Values, Methods, Obstacles, and Measures) model 20 years ago, and he says the "simplicity" of the framework has allowed the company to "raise the corporate consciousness of the entire organization."

You created the V2MOM framework on Day 1 of Salesforce and have been using them ever since. What are they and what are the main things they accomplish?

Everything we do at Salesforce starts with the V2MOM. We have a saying: "If it's not written down on a V2MOM, it's not going to happen."

I came up with the V2MOM concept during my time at Oracle in the mid-1990s when I was given responsibility to revamp our direct marketing programs. I had the budget, but little else in terms of a plan. I felt I needed more of a framework to help me identify key objectives, map out how to accomplish them, and assess how well we had achieved them. This was the impetus for creating the V2MOM, which stands for Vision, Values, Methods, Obstacles, and Measures.

Having a vision allows us to define our goals and what we want to do to achieve them. The values illuminate what is most important about that vision and can be expressed as the underlying principles and beliefs for the vision, in prioritized order. The methods are the practical actions that everyone needs to take to achieve the vision, and obstacles identify what could hold us back along the way. Finally, the measures specify the actual result we aim to achieve.

The V2MOM is an amazing alignment tool, cascading from the top of the company to the bottom. Every department and every employee drafts their own V2MOM at Salesforce. As a result, we are able to raise the corporate consciousness of the entire organization, with each part of the company and every individual understanding their role in achieving the vision.

Ultimately, the V2MOM creates a detailed map of where we want to go and provides a compass to direct us there.

What are the key elements to making V2MOM successful?

The biggest virtue of the V2MOM is its simplicity. It's not a complicated formula or lengthy process. The V2MOM framework encourages you to start with a blank sheet of paper, empty your mind, and bring a fresh perspective to any effort. And it works for every phase in the lifecycle of an organization. We used it when we were a start-up with a handful of people – and we use it today as a Fortune 500 company with more than 45,000 employees.

Every employee's V2MOM is published and accessible on our internal social network, *Chatter*. This creates a higher level of transparency and accountability, which is essential to our culture. We create a V2MOM when we acquire a company, create a new product, develop a new alliance, plan a new office or event, or modify our organizational structure. I've also found that whenever we've run into an insurmountable problem, it's because we didn't write it down and get our mind around it through the V2MOM process.

What are the implicit cultural impacts of using V2MOM? How would Salesforce's culture be different without them?

We've used the V2MOM to create our yearly plan across the company for more than 20 years. The V2MOM helps create a shared understanding of top-level priorities throughout our company and for all our stakeholders – employees, customers, partners, our communities, and shareholders. Every V2MOM incorporates our core values – trust, customer success, innovation, and equality – and provides our stakeholders with clarity and visibility into how they contribute to the company's overall success.

The Most Important Meeting of the Week

Once you've established your goals, they can then inform routine feedback, one-on-ones, and performance reviews. If you're just getting started with continuous feedback, start by making one-on-one meetings a priority for all managers and employees. One-on-ones are regular check-ins (we recommend weekly) that allow employees to raise issues with their managers, and allow managers to deliver feedback, praise employee successes, and help employees make adjustments where necessary. The one-on-one, as Ben Horowitz has said, is "the employee's meeting rather than the manager's meeting. This is the free-form meeting for all the pressing issues, brilliant ideas, and chronic frustrations that do not fit neatly into status reports, email, and other less personal and intimate mechanisms."[6]

In Lattice's 2020 State of People Strategy Survey, we asked HR leaders to tell us the importance of various feedback actions by employees and managers, and nearly 80 percent rated manager one-on-ones as *extremely* to *very* important. Another 75 percent rated ongoing manager feedback as *extremely* to *very* important. And of those who rated performance management as a "Top 3" initiative, 78 percent ranked "continuous feedback" as a priority for 2021.

One-on-ones are a regular opportunity for managers and direct reports to communicate. Employees drive the agenda, using this time to clear any roadblocks that they might be facing, get candid feedback from their manager, and discuss their broader goals. Managers, then, are better equipped to help their reports work through obstacles, bolster new ideas, and ensure that they are continuing down a path of success to helping the

---

[6]Ben Horowitz, "One on One," Andreesen Horowitz website (Aug 30, 2012), https://a16z.com/2012/08/30/one-on-one/

team meet its objectives. These free-form meetings should be a manager's most important meeting of the week (and prioritized as such), helping them and the company as a whole understand how employees feel about their work as well as their professional development. In virtual workspaces, these can become even more vital, ensuring that everyone remains on the same page even if they aren't in the same building.

While these meetings should always be employee-driven, managers should help guide the process, and bring up topics or questions concerning the employee as well. Encourage your direct reports to come prepared with an agenda of items they want to discuss, whether it is about their individual short- and long-term aspirations, job satisfaction, or constructive feedback about the company or the manager.

How to Run a Successful One-on-One Meeting

1. Make it about the employee.

It's important to remember that the meeting is about the employee – how they're feeling about work, what challenges they're facing, what ideas they have for improving the workplace, what personal problems they are experiencing, and how they want to grow their career and develop new skills. The employee should own the agenda and generally dictate the flow of the conversation.

2. Create a schedule and stick to it.

In the day-to-day routine, it's easy to think about one-on-ones as non-essential meetings, especially when they're not directly related to the bottom line or client work; but this is absolutely wrongheaded thinking. Remembering the advice of Andy Grove, managers must engage in high-leverage activities and one-on-ones are an essential tool to increase leverage. A 30-minute conversation with your employee can go a long way toward making sure that they're on track with OKRs and happy with their job. Put the time on your calendar and do your best not to cancel. If you can't make it, always reschedule. Not only will this show employees that they're a top priority, but it will also improve the work product and efficiency of the team.

3. Ask for an agenda.

Productive meetings take preparation, and one-on-ones are no exception. Since it's the employee's meeting, it's on them to prepare ahead of time. The employee should decide how they want to use their time with their manager.

4. Get them to open up.

Often, the conversation during a one-on-one stagnates – it was a slow week, so there were no big roadblocks, or the employee is an introvert. This is where it's time for the manager to start asking questions to draw out the key issues from employees.

Some questions that we've found to be effective are as follows:

- **Manager effectiveness**
  - In which areas of your work would you like more or less direction from me?
  - As your manager, what would you like me to stop, start, or continue doing?

- What do you need most from me right now?
- What challenges or roadblocks do you need help with?
- As your manager, what could I do more of to help you make progress toward your goals?
- **Effectiveness at work**
  - Do you feel overworked, underworked, or that you have the right workload?
  - What's your biggest problem right now? How are you feeling about it?
  - What do you want to do but don't feel like you have the time for?
  - What's an area of your work you want to improve? How can we work on that together?
  - What are your biggest concerns about your current project(s)?
  - What kind of communication or information do you wish you had more of?
- **Feedback and Development**
  - What is one aspect of your job you would like more help or coaching with?
  - Which areas would you like more feedback on from the team?
  - In what ways, if any, can I provide better or more feedback to help you succeed?
- **Short- and Long-Term Goals**
  - How can we help improve your day-to-day work?
  - How are you feeling about the project?

- What do you want to work on next quarter?
- A year from now, what do you want to have accomplished?
- Where do you see yourself in 5 years? 10 years? 20 years?
- **Company Improvement**
  - How can the team work better together? Where are we failing? Where are we succeeding?
  - What's your favorite/least favorite thing about the product?
  - How are you feeling about the company's future? Why do you say that?
  - If you were the CEO, what changes would you make?
- **Career Development**
  - Do you feel like we're helping to advance your career? What else can I be doing to help grow your career?
  - Do you feel like you're learning at work?
  - What projects are you most proud of? What do you want to work on next?
  - If you were not a [position], what do you want to be?
  - What's a professional development project that you'd like to pursue?

Another good tactic to get employees to open up is a change in scenery – we at Lattice are big fans of the walking one-on-one. If you're physically in the same office, go for a walk, get a cup of coffee, or just find a nice spot outdoors. This change will help managers build rapport and help even the most tight-lipped employees feel more comfortable.

5. Adjust your approach if your employees are remote workers.

Make sure that your one-on-ones don't fall away just because you're not all in the same office. These meetings are perhaps more important than before in keeping employees feeling connected and helping to build trust. Make sure that you both are using teleconference software and have cameras on, so that you can keep eye contact while having frank conversations about progress on goals, blockers, and morale.

Here are a few questions specific to monitoring remote workers' needs:

- Do you feel like you're able to maintain meaningful connections with what's happening at the company and your work friends?
- Do you feel like you're clear on priorities and goals right now?
- How are you feeling right now? What's your energy level? How is your stress level?
- Did you feel like you could take time for yourself during the workday this week?
- Do you have the hardware and software you need to work effectively?
- Are there specific projects or tasks that you feel are blocked or impacted by working remotely?
- Do you feel like you're able to take the time to focus on your professional development?

6. Take notes and follow up.

If you're running a successful one-on-one, then each week the manager will uncover different challenges and opportunities about the employee. Take notes and follow up on any issues. This shows the employees that you truly care about their concerns because you took the time (and remembered) to address their needs.

These meetings are the cornerstone of solid communication, and if conducted regularly, should ensure that employees aren't surprised by the time they reach their big review. While the principles and practice of one-on-ones may not change if they're being conducted in the conference room or over remote video chat, they take on perhaps even more importance when employees are working remotely – tethering workers to the organization's culture, even when they're not seeing their coworkers face-to-face.

Performance Reviews: The Big Checkup

If your managers are following the best practices of feedback culture, they've been keeping tabs on how each employee is performing against goals or OKRs and providing ongoing continuous feedback, course-correcting along the way. So, when it comes time for the big annual or bi-annual review, hopefully, everyone is completely prepared for what's to come.

The performance-review cycle is definitely heavy lifting for the HR team, but it's a process that will help reveal a ton of useful info about your people – from who are your top performers to which teams have great leadership, to where your employee-development challenges are.

To start the cycle, you'll need to make a few decisions:

Who should participate? Just managers reviewing employees? Will peers do reviews? Should managers get reviewed? Should employees review their own performance? At Lattice we believe in a true 360-feedback cycle, involving managers, employees, and peers,

How often should you do reviews? Lattice recommends reviews should be done twice a year or even quarterly. At minimum, reviews should be performed at least once a year as it creates an opportunity for you to get a full point-in-time picture of an individual's performance. We also understand that these full 360s are quite intensive, so we encourage our customers to (1) continuously solicit peer feedback (more on that following) and (2) run smaller review cycles outside of the 360 that facilitate ongoing performance and development conversations between managers and employees.

To give you a sense of how other companies handle reviews, let's look again at our State of People Strategy Survey. Eighty-nine percent of the HR professionals we surveyed said that they were running at least annual performance reviews, while 33 percent run semi-annual reviews, and 15 percent run quarterly reviews. As for who should participate, 36 percent said 360-degree feedback was their standard practice, 17 percent said they went with manager+peer feedback, 37 percent said "manager feedback only" was adequate, and the remainder went with some mix of manager with self-assessment or upward evaluation.

Next, you'll begin structuring the reviews themselves, which requires a few new decisions to make – which questions to ask and whether or not you choose to use ratings.

Performance review questions can really range widely from simple to complex and deep diving. Before drafting review questions, think about the broader category of employee qualities that you want to measure. For example:

Leadership: How well does an employee manage other people and motivate a group of individuals?

Project Management: How does this person approach completing their work product, and do they demonstrate strong time management skills when doing so?

Culture: How well does this person reflect the company values?

Career Development: What can this person do to improve their work product and working relationships at the company?

Impact: How much of a contribution does this person make to the organization?

Problem Solving: How does this person approach challenges? Do they employ creative ideas in solving problems?

Communication Skills: How well does this person interact with coworkers? Do they have a positive attitude, or are they always making negative comments?

Since you don't want to overwhelm your reviewers, you'll want to select those areas that matter most to you as an organization – either currently or what you'll need in the next phase of development. If you have competency matrices, or job paths, built out, consider cross-referencing your review questions with the competencies and competency themes that you have expectations around. And if not, more to come on that in later chapters.

Basic Performance Review Sample Questions

Are you looking for basic questions to use in your templates for 360-degree reviews? Here are a handful of sample questions for the four basic review types.

Employee Review: For a manager to evaluate their direct report's performance.

- What's an area where you've seen this person excel?
- What's an area you'd like to see this person improve?
- To what extent did this person meet their performance goals?
- How well does this person prioritize and manage their workload?
- How well does this person communicate with others?
- Provide an example of one company value this person brought to life.

Upward Manager Review: For an employee to evaluate their manager's performance.

- Is your manager action-oriented? How well do they drive results?
- How well does your manager support your professional and personal growth?
- Does your manager accept feedback? Does your manager communicate well?

Self-Review: For an employee to evaluate their own performance.

- What accomplishments are you most proud of?
- To what extent did you meet your goals for the year?
- How well do you prioritize and manage your workload?
- How well do you listen to and communicate with others?
- What do you think you should do differently next year?
- Provide an example of one company value you brought to life and how.

Peer Review: For employees to evaluate their colleague's performance.

- How would you rate the quality of the employee's work?
- How does this person embody our company values?
- What have been their successes? What are their challenges?
- If you could give this person one piece of constructive advice to make them more effective in their role, what would you say?

Next, you'll need to decide whether you'll use numerical ratings or open feedback fields for how your people will execute their reviews. Many companies prefer using ratings. Anyone who's used Yelp to pick a restaurant for dinner or perused user ratings on Amazon can understand that there's nothing more black-and-white than a rating scale. Whether you're using a 3-point, 5-point, or letter-grade system, you'll see right away who your company's managers view as the top performers, and they'll be sorted into ranked lists (especially if you're using a performance software tool like Lattice). Depending on the number of rating variables, you can parse those high performers based on specific skills or goals. And using numerical ratings mean gathering quantitative data that can help HR teams and leaders feel confident in decisions around raises and promotions.

Another advantage for using ratings: it's often very hard to get quality feedback from managers, especially during busy review periods. Writing out a review is time-consuming and, for some, extremely difficult. Data shows that managers struggle when ratings aren't an option. According to 2016 research by CEB (now Gartner), "Manager conversation quality declines by 14 percent because managers struggle to explain to employees how they performed in the past and what steps to take to improve future performance," and "less than 5 percent of managers can effectively manage employees without [ratings.]"[7]

On the other hand, many HR leaders feel that assigning numbers discourages insightful feedback, focusing on the score instead of a true review. And if your company is trying to stay true to a "culture of feedback," keep in mind that detailed feedback full of examples and advice versus a simple grade or star rating could go a long way to helping the actual improvement you may want to see from your people.

Looking again at our People Strategy Survey, just over 36 percent of HR pros said that they relied on an equal amount of ratings and comments for a balanced view, nearly 26 percent

---

[7]Jackie Wiles, "The Real Impact on Employees of Removing Performance Ratings," (*Smarter With Gartner*, Aug 15, 2019), https://www.gartner.com/smarterwithgartner/corporate-hr-removing-performance-ratings-is-unlikely-to-improve-performance/

leaned heavily on comments with a few ratings, 21 percent were mostly reliant on ratings with a small amount of comments. Only 14 percent said that they preferred all comments and no ratings, and a tiny 1.9 percent said that they only went with ratings.

Once you roll out reviews, make sure that you have a plan to ensure that there's high participation through a strong communication plan, a generous timeline with a lot of heads-up and reminders, training for newbies, and setting goals to rally around. Once reviews are closed, then begins the hard job of analyzing results to make decisions around development budgets, promotions, and even compensation.

Remember to make time to calibrate your review scores. Why calibrate? Scores can vary widely based on the reviewer since people across your company are interpreting your grading system differently. A practical way to handle calibration is to form committees of managers' managers who understand their people's scoring styles and can help provide context and guidance on how to interpret and level scores.

And finally, you'll need to conclude the reviews cycle across your company through a series of manager-employee meetings where they can discuss the results of the review, as well as address the question of raises or promotions. Or if this is a mid-year cycle that's more about development, be ready with action plans for how you can support learning new skills or, how to step up and meet expectations.

Delivering Feedback: Tough Conversations and Praise

If the regular flow of communication is strong, these reviews should go smoothly. Just remember, feedback should be balanced. We've all experienced the two extremes of management: the critic manager you only hear from when you screw up and the conflict-averse manager who wants to be loved above all and never delivers tough truths. I'm here to say that both of these managers are not helping your business because they're not helping your people.

Let's start with positive feedback, because when we think of "feedback," we often tend to think of the negative kind: things we could have done better or differently or mistakes that need correcting. But giving employees praise for a job well done goes a long way to retaining top performers and motivating employees to do amazing work. Just to list a few stats around recognition:

- An OC Tanner study showed that 79 percent of people who quit their jobs cite "lack of appreciation" as their reason for leaving.
- A Zenger & Folkman survey found that 69 percent of employees said they would work harder if they felt their efforts were better recognized.
- And a Towers Watson study showed that organizations that place a heavy emphasis on praising and recognizing employee achievements showed engagement scores increase by nearly 60 percent.

At Lattice, one of our most popular product features, both internally as well as with our customers, is our Praise feature that lets employees and managers share positive feedback either privately or publicly (see Figure 3.2). Public praise sent through Lattice sends a shout-out through a company-wide Slack channel or via another public chat platform, even allowing users to tag the feedback with what company values the "win" represents and allowing other employees to add on with emojis or replies.

One thing to keep in mind: not everyone enjoys public recognition! Managers should make it part of their onboarding practice of getting to know employees to find out whether they prefer praise publicly or privately. The last thing you want to do is to make recognition uncomfortable.

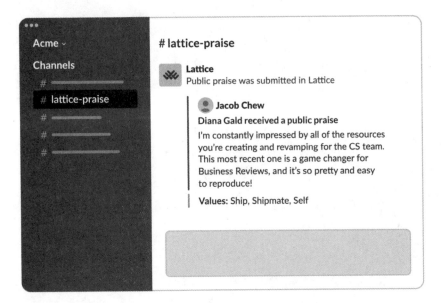

FIGURE 3.2

Six Times Managers Should Give Praise to Their Employees

There's never a bad time to give employees some positive recognition, but these six key moments demand that managers go out of their way to show up with some praise.

Note: All of these moments could be handled publicly or privately.

1. When They Get Hired/When They're Onboarding

An employee's first few weeks are crucial to their understanding of the company culture, the expectations of the job, and their future performance.

Sample script: "You're doing great." "We're so glad you're here!" "Thanks for taking over these million little things..."

2. When They Get Promoted

When your employee finally gets elevated into a position that they've worked hard to achieve, it's important to celebrate that big career move.

Sample script: "This is long overdue! Thanks to your work in X and Y. I know you'll be great at this."

3. When They Go Out of Their Comfort Zone

Your employee has been trying on a new role or took on challenging new responsibilities. Giving them praise at this moment means that you want them to know you have their back.

Sample script: "I saw X working on Y, and I was really delighted to see how hard they were working on something new. You're doing great. Remember, it's a process. Keep going!"

4. After a Big Launch That They Helmed

Even if it's something your team has been working on for a while, show them that their leadership helped you and the company.

Sample script: "I know that was a lot of work and a lot of little details to juggle at once. You did a great job, and we really appreciate it."

5. When They Go Above and Beyond Expectations

They took on a task or project and went above and beyond in a way that delighted and surprised you.

Sample script: "X went above and beyond expectations on project Y, and I'm beyond impressed!"

6. When They Have an Anniversary at the Company

It's absolutely on managers to be the first person to acknowledge and celebrate that moment for their employees. This shows that you appreciate them and want to keep working with them.

Sample script: "Congratulations to X for his/her/their Xth anniversary with [company]! X has been a great addition to our team. They were indispensable in projects A, B, and C [write as much as you like – this is a big moment]."

But even in a good feedback culture, things sometimes need a little extra work. Perhaps you notice a pattern in an employee's work, be it a behavior that is getting in the way or a similar mistake being made again and again. Maybe you notice them struggling a bit, and some constructive criticism could help them develop into the employee you know they can become. In any case, constructive feedback is the heart of a good company culture. It can certainly help increase productivity and efficiency, but it can also help the employee grow.

Constructive feedback – that is, raising where someone's behavior, output, or result didn't match your expectations in some way – should be deployed regularly and should always be delivered as part of a conversation. As Rabois, the investor, once told me: "People tend to procrastinate about it, they tend to defer – almost like writing an essay in college – because it takes a lot of work to do well, and the news isn't always pleasant, therefore you tend to hope it goes away but it almost never does." Like the old-school performance reviews we discussed above, we all have that classic image in our heads of the stern boss lecturing employees about productivity or coming down hard on them for every little mistake. But that's neither the most effective nor the most reasonable way to get the most out of your employees. In these difficult conversations, it's important to make it clear that you and the employee are on the same team – approaching the issue as a problem that you can solve together, rather than some deficiency that they need to correct on their own. This will help ensure that the focus remains on the challenge at hand and help both the manager and the employee work together to come up with a strategy to correct course.

If you're noticing some of those common scenarios where you want to deliver some constructive feedback, here are some starter scripts to initiate the conversation:

When You're Noticing a Pattern

When an employee is constantly making the same mistake or has a bad work habit, you have to address it with specific examples. You have the fact that it's a repeated behavior to support why you're bringing it up, but you can't let them continue the bad behavior only to spring it on them months later during their performance review.

> *Sample script:* "I've noticed that you've been late to the morning meeting several times this month. We understand you have a difficult commute, but this can be really disruptive to your coworkers. Is there something going on that makes it hard for you to be on time?"

For Developmental Purposes

When you notice an employee is struggling with a skill or can't complete a task, constructive feedback can help you get to the root of the issue and find a solution. Perhaps they were never properly trained, or they feel afraid to ask for help. Feedback can help you tackle the situation together and improve.

Sample script: "How are you feeling about creating that quarterly report? I am highly motivated to make you successful with it. What can I do to ensure you have everything you need?"

To Manage Workload

Sometimes, a team member's workload isn't realistic, or they feel strained and unsupported. Before the situation reaches levels of burnout, take time for a feedback conversation with them; many people who feel burned out don't know how to bring it up. Then you list steps to help them reset and move forward.

Sample script: "How are you feeling about your workload lately? Does it seem manageable to you, or do you feel like you're being spread too thin?"

These conversations can be difficult. But the alternative to clear communication is always worse. Kim Scott, an advisor to Dropbox, Twitter, and other top Silicon Valley firms, has an example she uses to support what she calls *Radical Candor*.[8] She famously talks about an employee named "Bob." He was, she recalls, charming and funny and personable – an enjoyable employee to have around. There was just one problem: his work wasn't any good. "His work just absolutely sucked," she told me once. But rather than give him constructive feedback or put him on a performance improvement plan, she said, she gave what she called "head-fake praise." "This is a great start," she remembered telling him. When it became clear, after nearly a year of this, that his performance wasn't improving, she realized that she was going to lose other team members if she did not let Bob go. "I sat down and had a conversation that I should have had with Bob

[8]Kim Scott, "How to Give Candid Feedback," Lattice website (March 13, 2017), https://lattice.com/interview/kim-scott-how-to-give-candid-feedback

months ago," she told me. After describing his sub-par perfor-mance, she recalled, Bob stood up: "Why didn't you tell me?" he asked her.

"I realized in that moment that I had failed Bob," she told me. Not only did she fail to provide feedback to Bob about his performance, but she hadn't allowed him to communicate reg-ular feedback to her about any support she may have needed. Moreover, the work environment was apparently such that Bob's colleagues never brought up his sub-par performance.

This is an extreme example, perhaps, but it illustrates the importance of a strong feedback culture. When open communi-cation is encouraged, fostered, and maintained, successes can be reinforced, and shortcomings can be met head-on. Problems that otherwise would have been allowed to fester, like the pitcher who just can't seem to get anybody out, can be addressed as they arise. And whether things are going well or need some improvement, reviews won't take employees by surprise.

Key Points

- Performance feedback should not come as a surprise – it should be consistent, continuous, and free-flowing.
- Goals make an excellent foundation for setting expectations, giving feedback, and measuring performance.
- A healthy feedback culture involves routine communica-tion, employee-driven one-on-one meetings, and perfor-mance reviews.
- Positive feedback goes a long way to retaining top perform-ers and motivating employees to do amazing work.
- When it's time for tough conversations, however, honest, open communication is crucial.

CHAPTER

4

Building Engagement

For any company, a strong culture is the glue – for both the good times and the bad. When things are going great, a strong company culture makes them seem even better. When things get tough, it helps to soften the blow. That same strong company culture helps attract and retain talented employees and brings the whole organization together, from the top executives in the C-suite to individual contributors. In other words, culture unites the entire company behind a single, shared purpose. A vibrant, supportive, and engaging culture is an important part of any company's success.

But every company's culture is unique, much like each individual's personality, and there are many ways to attain a good one. Maybe your company's culture is strong because of transparent leadership. Maybe it's defined by your company's priority of hiring nontraditional candidates. The exact components of a good company culture may be hard to define, but you know it when you see it.

As I mentioned in the introduction, "Why Your Company Should Put People First," I founded Lattice, in part, because of what I came to see as failures of company culture at Teespring; the notion that great company culture helps attract and retain top talent, and can get the most out of everybody in the organization, was a big part of the foundation we built at Lattice. Facing a moment of crisis at Lattice, like other companies during the coronavirus pandemic, further deepened my sense of what culture means and provides. It doesn't just bring people together when things are running smoothly; it also binds the company together when things get rough.

So how can you establish a good organizational culture? And how can you maintain it?

The Benefits of Culture Go Both Ways

As I discussed earlier, culture refers to the values, beliefs, and attitudes that serve as the north star for everyone at an organization – from the executive level on down. A company's culture is a huge part of what makes a company attractive to prospective hires, and all of the things that connect employees to their work. It helps make work meaningful for employees and aids in the productivity of organizations.

According to recent surveys, nearly half of job seekers say company culture is an important factor that they consider when evaluating prospective workplaces, and virtually all say it is at least a consideration. More than a third of workers say they'd pass on their dream job if it wasn't a culture fit – and 15 percent say that they have turned down a job offer because of the workplace culture of their prospective employer.

And if you're trying to attract the highest-caliber talent to hire for your organization, great culture builds a great brand for you as an employer. Just think of the companies that are the places where everyone wants to work. They all have a great employer brand, and they have that because they have renowned cultures.

Speaking at Lattice's Resources for Humans conference, we asked Margo Downs, HR consultant and former chief people officer at Stitch Fix, who has also led People teams at Lululemon and Starbucks, what it takes to build the kind of culture and brand that people seek out and makes you a "hot company." She said:

> Like any kind of a reputation, right now, you actually already have an employer brand. People are talking about your company as a place to work, whether you're managing what that is or not. The employer brand to me is your culture made manifest externally, and it should be authentic to who you are and what your culture is. It's allowing you to attract the types of people that you actually want to attract who are the correct people to really take your company forward. There are a lot of really great companies that do that really well, because they do a really good job of creating a culture that is very aligned with what they're up to as a business.

Studies also show that employees are significantly more likely to leave companies if the culture is lacking, just as I did when the culture at Teespring turned toxic. In those early days, I saw the company and its environment as brimming with potential. We had a clear mission, we shared values, and we were engaged with our work, fostering friendships and a strong sense of community along the way. But within a couple of years, things changed for the worse. The mission grew confused, connections between teams and employees began to fray, and people's interactions became wracked with tension and anxiety. Such a culture makes it difficult for companies to retain employees who otherwise might stay. Even Millennials – who have a reputation for leapfrogging from job to job, supposedly lacking the company loyalty of the generations that preceded them – actually do not prefer to job-hop. More than half of working Millennials say they would like to stay at one company for 20 years or more. This suggests that it's not a lack of commitment that drives them from workplace to workplace; instead, I would propose that it's their values that prioritize a strong organizational culture and sense of community.

This makes sense. We spend so much of our time at work, whether we're in the office or working remotely; research from the 2020 Global Culture Report suggests that making those everyday experiences more positive, inspiring, and psychologically safe can improve both the employee experience and productivity.

Indeed, the benefits of strong culture go both ways. While that sense of community helps employees feel more engaged, that engagement in turn improves productivity company-wide. A 2001 Gallup survey, "What Your Disaffected Workers Cost," found that nearly two in 10 workers in the United States "not only fail to be enthralled by their work but are fundamentally disconnected from it."[1] These actively disengaged workers tend to be less productive at work, are more prone to missing time, and report being more stressed, unhappy, and insecure in what they do. This comes at an enormous cost for businesses; that same survey found that actively disengaged workers cost the US economy about $300 billion – and that was almost 20 years ago. A strong company culture keeps employees engaged; engaged employees work harder, are more loyal, and are less likely to leave. As Asana's Anna Binder once told me, "Building an amazing culture is a means to an end." She continued, "The whole

---

[1]"What Your Disaffected Workers Cost," *Business Journal* (March 15, 2001), https://news.gallup.com/businessjournal/439/what-your-disaffected-workers-cost.aspx

point of building a culture where people are empowered and happy is because in that environment, amazing employees will do great things to help further your business."[2]

We had an employee who, before coming to Lattice, had been a high-performing sales representative for a different company. I'm actually under-selling it a little bit: He wasn't *just* a high performer; he was one of the company's top performers. He was doing fantastically well, hitting all his goals, and making good money. From the outside, it would seem that everything for him at the company was great.

However, he felt a lack of support from the culture and zero help from the managers. To him, all it seemed that the three or four managers he cycled through over the course of a year cared about were his numbers. He didn't feel that they cared about his career goals or anything else about him. Culture and community mattered a great deal to him, and he felt that was lacking. So, even though he was doing well for himself, he was unhappy and ultimately quit to take a job with us.

This came as a surprise to the company he left. Most of the time, when we think of the top performers at an organization, we assume that they must be happy. We don't imagine them quitting. But this shows how important it is for a company to see the employee as a whole person and to offer them more than compensation. Companies need to build support structures and community, a culture that truly cares about employee engagement and happiness.

This may be especially true when it comes to small businesses and start-ups. Fred Stevens-Smith, cofounder and CEO of Rainforest QA once told me that "culture is the most important

---

[2]Anna Binder, "Anna Binder on How Asana Built Silicon Valley's Leading Company Culture," Lattice website (June 21, 2017), https://lattice.com/interview/anna-binder-asana

thing to any start-up," allowing smaller and newer businesses to compete against comparatively large, better-resourced companies. "I think what building a successful company comes down to is about hiring the best people and retaining the best people," Stevens-Smith told me. "And for me, that is the purpose of culture. The purpose of culture is to have a very robust framework within which you can hire and retain the best people."

Culture Doesn't Just Appear. So How Do You Build It?

Now that we've determined that good company culture is important, both in good times and in bad, how do we *build* it?

It can be easy to think that a healthy organizational culture just happens magically, without any effort at all. This couldn't be more untrue. Culture is something companies must consciously foster and work to maintain, or else it will fast go downhill. In a way, culture builds on itself. It takes engaged employees to help establish organizational culture; that culture in turn helps employees remain engaged. This is why regular engagement surveys are a great way of ensuring that employees are plugged into the company culture and satisfied with their day-to-day experience. If the reviews we discussed in the last chapter are the "checkup" of employee *performance*, these surveys are the "checkup" of their *engagement*.

When we recently surveyed over 570 HR and People leaders for our State of People Strategy Survey, a whopping 72 percent of them said that annual engagement surveys were a big part of their standard practice for keeping on top of how employees were feeling.

Conducted two to four times per year, these are surveys of 25–50 questions meant to take the temperature of your.

organizational culture and establish a benchmark for future check-ins. Engagement surveys empower company leaders to troubleshoot any shortcomings in company culture and to institute positive changes that will improve retention, employee satisfaction, and organizational morale. Conducting them also sends a message to employees that you care about their day-to-day experience and job satisfaction, and that you are committed to creating the best work environment you can.

To begin the process, it's important to establish the area of focus for the survey. While some of the questions should be broad enough to gauge an employee's feelings about the company's culture as a whole, a good engagement survey will consist mostly of more pointed, unambiguous, and deeper questions designed to assess areas that leaders and managers have identified as potential problems that could negatively affect engagement – otherwise called "drivers" of engagement. During this brainstorming process, company leaders should consult managers to get a sense of issues that they may be seeing among their reports. Managers should have a finger on the pulse of the company and their teams and will be able to identify areas of engagement that may need attention or improvement. Past engagement surveys, as well as exit interviews, can also be instructive.

Once you have developed a list of potential problems, narrow the focus of the Engagement Survey, keeping the following questions in mind:

1. Is this a problem that we can solve in a reasonable time frame?
2. How often does the problem occur?
3. How costly or problematic is the issue?
4. Does the company have the resources to solve the problem?
5. What is the main benefit of solving the problem?

These questions will help you assess the scope of the issue, the viability of solving it, and the priority of addressing it. Once you've determined the most pressing and solvable issue, dig deep into the drivers of the problem. The idea here is not only to focus on the surface of the issue but to get to the root of it. One way of doing this is the Five Whys Analysis developed in the mid-twentieth century by legendary Toyota executive Taiichi Ohno.

Seeking to eliminate waste at the company, the story goes that Ohno questioned senior management about components the company was stockpiling at great expense to the bottom line. To each of their responses, he would continually ask, "Why?" until he eventually got to the underlying causes of the problem. The system worked, and Ohno is now known as the father of Toyota's innovative production system. We can apply the same principle – asking "why" five times until we've gone well below the symptoms of the problem at hand, and found our way to a diagnosis.

Suppose that you notice a trend when you talk to managers and look at past engagement surveys and exit surveys: a lot of employees seem burned out – a common enough problem that could have many different underlying causes and, thus, many different solutions. The first why you ask might reveal that the workload has become unrealistic. That leads to the next question: Why has the workload grown so untenable? The answer: We have gained 50 new clients over the past year, but only four new employees. This kind of probing can be a painstaking process but can dig down to the root cause or causes of the problem that you're attempting to address and point to a hypothesis about the possible issues your employees are facing.

Once you have this foundation, you can begin crafting questions. Good engagement driver survey questions are pointed and unambiguous; they ask just one thing at a time, are worded neutrally, and directly relate to something you can change or improve upon. They should also allow employees to comment if they see fit. They can be open-ended questions, or they can be agree/disagree statements like the following:

How to Write Engagement Driver Survey Questions

In an engagement survey, what you ask about and how you ask it are important. While positioned as yes-or-no statements, these standardized questions are developed to do the following:

- Be pointed and unambiguous
- Ask about one thing at a time
- Be worded neutrally
- Ask about something you can actually change or improve

We have several categories based on engagement survey research, and all questions are rated on a Likert scale (strongly disagree, disagree, neutral, agree, and strongly agree) to help gauge how intensely an employee feels about a topic. Keep in mind that making the survey easy to complete and not too long will help ensure participation.

Self-Efficacy

Workers need to feel that they have a certain degree of autonomy at work; but they also have to feel supported.

1. **I can list concrete steps I need to take in order to move up in my organization within the next year.**

This is a direct question that can help you determine whether employees feel they can grow at your company and whether they have a clear vision of their trajectory there.

2. **I can see myself growing and developing my career in this company.*** When employees believe that they have a way to grow at the company, they are more invested in the company's future.

3. **There is adequate company support for my skill development.** This question addresses personal goals by asking employees to gauge how well the company supports the acquisition of skills that *they* want to learn, not something prescribed by a manager.

4. **This organization really inspires the very best in me when it comes to job performance.** When employees believe that they are being pushed to do their best work, they are fully engaged in their development and production at a company.

5. **I am excited about the majority of my work projects/ customers.** If employees aren't excited about the work they are doing, they are definitely not getting fulfillment from their jobs. Adding an always/sometimes/ never scale helps managers identify how engaged employees are in the work they are doing.

6. **I have all the tools or resources I need to consistently do my job well.** This can help you gauge whether employees feel they have all they need to succeed in their role, or whether they haven't been given the necessary materials/equipment, or feel overworked or overwhelmed.

Fit and Belonging

If an employee doesn't feel like they are strongly part of or "belong" to a company's culture, they'll lose motivation and become disengaged.

7. **I find that my values and the organization's values are similar.** * When employees can see their core beliefs reflected in the place they work, they are more likely to find personal satisfaction working there.

8. **I feel like I belong in this company.** * This is a powerful indicator of whether or not something is awry, especially when you analyze your results to look at how different groups feel.

9. **I plan to still be at this company in two years.** This is an indirect yet powerful way to gauge happiness with personal goals. Those who are not planning long-term employment with you will not believe that their personal goals align with what your company is offering them.

10. **The organization's mission consistently inspires me to do my best work.** What your company has set out to do in the world can make or break employee engagement. Knowing whether or not that mission motivates your employees can help you determine how they view the company on the whole.

11. **My work style is supported by my colleagues and manager.** * By asking this question, you'll learn a lot about which teams, departments, and employees feel supported at the company and which do not.

* Indicates that these are questions found in Lattice's engagement survey question bank offered to Lattice customers.

12. **I see a clear tie between the company's mission and my individual job.** It helps to feel that your job is important and to be able to connect your role to the purpose of the company itself – when an employee feels that their day-to-day work feeds into that larger goal helps them stay engaged.

Team Culture, Team Learning, and Work Relationships

One of the biggest elements contributing to employee engagement has to do with their team – the work they do, the way they work, and the friendships they've made.

13. **I learn a lot from my coworkers.*** Collaboration depends on employees understanding how other people work and what they're working on. Employees being open to learning from their coworkers also indicates a degree of mutual respect, which increases productivity.

14. **We regularly take time to figure out ways to improve our team's work processes.*** When a team is constantly refining their processes, that's a great sign that people are internally aligned and committed to working toward a goal.

15. **My team has clear and prioritized objectives.** This question can be a great way to dig into the different segments of your company. If a certain team lacks alignment or goals, it can affect that segment's overall connection to the company, but you won't know the team alignment is the reason unless you ask.

16. **My supervisor or someone at work seems to care about me.*** We spend the majority of our life at work, and employees flourish when they feel connected to the people with whom they work.

17. **My coworkers have the skills and expertise to do their jobs well.*** This indicates the level of trust an employee has in their coworkers' ability to do their work.

18. **My department is consistently given all of the information we need to execute our objectives.** This question can help you determine if there are deficiencies in communication from department to department, or along the chain of command.

19. **How would you describe working at your company in three words? (comment box).*** If you want to know how your employees feel about your culture, the best thing to do is to let them use their own words.

20. **If I could change one thing about our company culture, it would be (comment box).** This is an important follow-up to asking about the culture. For example, you might feel that "competitive" is an important aspect of your company culture. But if many employees list "competitiveness" as something they would change; you've gained insight into a disconnect between employees and management.

Overall Engagement

A job can be stimulating but unsatisfying. Asking about engagement in particular is critical to delve into how invested they are in their role.

* Indicates that these are questions found in Lattice's engagement survey question bank offered to Lattice customers.

21. **I am proud to be an employee at my company.** A broad question like this is a gut check for your company. It can help you clearly delineate how employees are feeling, even if some of the more nuanced or personal questions about job satisfaction show mixed results.

22. **I would refer a friend or a family member to this company.** If an employee would recommend that a friend or a family member work for the company, they are satisfied with their employer. This is very similar to the question used in evaluating eNPS, which we'll cover later in this chapter.

23. **I feel exhausted in the morning at the thought of another day at work.*** Satisfaction is more than just an overall good feeling about a job; it also means that people are excited about the work they are doing.

24. **I generally believe that my workload is reasonable for my role.** Employees aren't likely to say they feel overwhelmed for fear it might reflect poorly on them, but framing the question to be about their workload will better enable them to be candid.

25. **I feel recognized for my hard work and successes at work.** If an employee believes that they are not being recognized, they may not derive satisfaction from their work. If all of the other questions indicate that people are generally happy, but engagement is low, asking whether they feel recognized is a way to frame their problem more holistically.

Psychological Safety

Without strong psychological safety, employees won't take risks, and neither employees nor companies can innovate and grow.

26. **When I approach my manager with a problem, I trust that they will listen.** By asking something that is both specific and personal, you can learn a great deal about the responder. Gauging a degree of trust is an excellent way to discuss communication without being vague.

27. **I know who to talk to if I am having a problem that is not in my manager's domain.** If an employee doesn't know who to talk to, then communication is at zero, which is a big problem that often goes unnoticed.

28. **I feel that there is at least one person at work who supports and encourages my development.** It's vital that employees feel that there's someone in their corner; someone who is invested in their growth and who genuinely cares about them.

29. **Members of this team can bring up problems and tough issues.*** Asking if a team communicates well is tricky because it can be broken down in many ways – from one-on-one talks to project meetings. But asking whether anyone can bring up a tough issue helps determine whether the team feels empowered to speak up.

30. **I am comfortable sharing my opinion at an all-hands meeting.** Asking this will tell you how confident employees feel about opening up to the company. If someone strongly disagrees, that's an indication that you need to probe the problem further; for example, is it because they don't expect people to listen or because they're not sure what avenue to follow to bring an opinion up?

Management

Asking about management can tell you two main things: whether your managers are acting in accordance with your policies, and whether your management policies are working.

* Indicates that these are questions found in Lattice's engagement survey question bank offered to Lattice customers.

31. **My manager demonstrates an interest in my well-being.** While the responses to this question can vary by manager, if the majority of respondents don't feel their managers care, it's more than a case-by-case problem – it's a systematic lack of support from the top down.

32. **My manager sets clear expectations for my performance.** This is a great way to assess how effectively a manager communicates with their reports.

33. **I feel comfortable giving feedback to my manager.** If an employee can be honest with their manager about the manager's performance, that is an indicator that the two have built a strong working relationship.

34. **My manager has the technical expertise required to effectively manage me.*** This is a good question to ask when a manager is going through all the right motions – the one-on-ones, the public praise, the problem solving – but a team is still disengaged. Even the best-intentioned manager will fail if they don't have the tools to support their team.

35. **I feel comfortable asking for help if I do not have the skills required to meet my goals (+ comment box).** Is their manager not receptive? Do they feel that a time crunch on their productivity leaves no opportunity to ask questions?

* Indicates that these are questions found in Lattice's engagement survey question bank offered to Lattice customers.

When conducting engagement surveys, trust is key. Be open with employees about the purpose of the survey and make it so that results are either fully anonymous or anonymized of any identifiable information to ensure honesty. It's also important that it be easy to understand and, ultimately, complete; the more employees who participate, the more precisely it will capture your company's organizational culture. Most crucially, you should be clear with employees about how important the survey is and how the results will be used by management to assess and solve potential problems.

Ideally, the results will give you a big picture view of your company culture. But it's also important to drill down even deeper and analyze the surveys more specifically. While the broad trends that become apparent in the results will surely give you a general sense of how employees at your company feel about the culture and their day-to-day work, examining the results on a more granular level will provide insights you may have missed at first. Suppose your survey results indicate that three-quarters of your employees overall are pleased and engaged with the company culture – that would be an excellent sign, suggesting a generally strong culture and a plugged-in workforce

But if your survey collects demographic or manager data by taker (and later anonymized), you can break those numbers down by cross-section to find problem areas that the overall data glosses over. For example, if 75 percent of employees overall have a positive view of company culture, but only, say, 50 percent of your employees of color say the same, it tells a different story. Similarly, you might find that a given department or subset of teams has a disproportionately lower overall score, in which case you would want to focus on those teams when coming up with action items. Digging deeper into the data allows you to ensure that all employees and all departments are feeling supported and included in the company culture. (See Figure 4.1.)

In addition to probing deeper into the data, also be sure to take time to go through employees' thoughts and suggestions on open-ended questions. The agree/disagree answers to

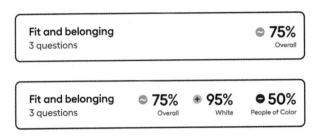

FIGURE 4.1

the questions you crafted will point toward trends in the data, but their written responses will add nuance. For instance, the responses you might get to an agree/disagree question like "This organization's mission consistently inspires me to do my best work" will be telling. But having an employee share why or why not can help point to what's working in the company culture or what solutions might be needed to address any shortcomings.

Finally, it's important to share with your employees what you took away from the survey. This is crucial because it emphasizes to employees your commitment to taking the survey outcome seriously and demonstrates that you are receptive to their concerns and suggestions. Company culture isn't established through engagement surveys alone. But engagement surveys allow company leaders to ensure that the organization is living out its values and that all employees are aligned.

A great example of this is Lattice customer ParkHub, which turned to surveys during the coronavirus crisis when they noticed that the stress of rapidly changing business priorities was deeply affecting their employees. The company rolled out Lattice's "crisis response survey" first, using our set of pre-populated questions that address how employees are feeling during times of intense change.

While the survey was initially met with some nervousness among employees, ParkHub made it clear that the survey was confidential and that the team needed honest opinions in order to provide the best support.

"Anytime we've made changes, people are concerned with why we made them," said Nick Schanbaum, ParkHub's general counsel and chief of staff. "The logic behind the survey is that we need to know if we're doing the right thing – and we need to know right now. We can't waste a month with employees being unhappy and suffering in silence." In the end, they had an overwhelmingly high response rate, with all but 3 of over 60 employees responding.

In the end, the survey helped ParkHub plan out initiatives that were extremely well received by its employees. One example was that they looked at the data and saw that employees were working themselves ragged. That negative result raised a flag for ParkHub's management, and they understood that they needed to lead by example themselves. "None of the leadership was taking time off," says Schanbaum. "We had a realization that we weren't practicing what we were preaching, and so we couldn't expect other people to do it."

ParkHub's chief revenue officer would attend some early morning meetings while hiking in the hills; its president and chief revenue officer would highlight their boxing and powerlifting regimens to the team. Schanbaum said he would to attend some of the company's virtual culture-building events while grilling or splashing in an inflatable pool with his daughter. "The message quickly took. Once we made it clear how seriously we took self-care – and kept reinforcing it – our team started to make time for themselves. Planned bike rides and video game sessions started showing up on calendars."

Encouraged by these results, ParkHub is building surveys into its ongoing HR strategy. "I want to run this survey all the time," said Schanbaum. "I want to show our team that we are asking for feedback, and then go and do the things that they say they want us to do. You can't do the right thing unless you ask the right questions. You need a process that is part of a system."

Schanbaum added: "I want to know if employees understand where we're headed as a company. I want to know if our high performers are happy or unhappy; because if they're unhappy, we've got to fix that. As with everything, it all comes back to bringing value to our stakeholders, but at the end of the day, strong margins can't stand up to a weak culture."

What Is eNPS?

"How likely are you to recommend this business to a friend?" Companies have used the *Net Promoter Score (NPS)* methodology since 2003 to measure sentiment toward just about anything, from software to burritos.

With engaging and retaining top performers top of mind for most companies, HR departments have brought the concept of NPS to the workplace. The resulting metric, *employee Net Promoter Score (eNPS)*, has risen to importance on many HR analytics dashboards.

Calculating eNPS

When asked if they'd recommend your company as a place to work to a friend, employees respond using a scale of 0 (not at all likely) to 10 (extremely likely). While that sounds intuitive enough, calculating eNPS isn't a matter of averaging scores. Based on their feedback, respondents are grouped into one of three categories: promoters, detractors, and passives.

So, what do these categories mean?

Promoters

Promoters, or employees who score 9–10, are your company's greatest advocates. They're a major asset to your employer brand and recruiting efforts. These employees are more likely to share job postings on LinkedIn and within their network – they are essentially your company's brand ambassadors.

Detractors

Detractors aren't just apathetic about the company's prospects for success, they could hurt your brand in the long term. These individuals are unhappy enough to "gripe to friends, relatives, acquaintances – anyone who will listen," wrote Fred Reichheld, NPS's creator. Detractors score anywhere between 0 and 6, meaning that they account for over half of the rubric.

Passives

Passives, otherwise known as "passive respondents," are neutral. They might like working at your company, but not enough to actively refer friends to it. If you could sum up their feelings as a LinkedIn status, they're "open to opportunities," but not actively looking. Scores from 7–8 are considered passive and won't factor into your final calculation.

Once you have your survey responses, subtract your percentage of detractors from your percentage of promoters. This calculation will yield your company's eNPS. Keep in mind that an eNPS can be as high as +100 (the absolute best) or –100 (the absolute worst). Intuitively, anything below 0 is cause for concern. If you use Lattice, our employee survey software will handle this calculation automatically.

What NPS Measures (and What It Doesn't)

Management thinkers love "silver bullet" approaches to work. After all, it's why NPS was billed as the ultimate question when it was first introduced. However, while it's a useful tool for measuring employee satisfaction and loyalty, HR experts warn against using it solely to get a read on engagement. After all, it's a measure of faith in the business, not individual happiness or productivity. In that respect, it's a great metric for recruiters to track as they look to roll out or update referral programs.

Olivia Bair, director of global HR at Instapage, explained that she appreciates the value HR teams get out of eNPS at a recent Lattice conference. But for it to be really meaningful, she thinks it needs to be part of a much broader employee survey strategy:

> It's hard to sum up everything we do into just one question. We're about engagement. We're about career development, performance management, goal setting, and everything else that's part of that employee lifecycle.[3]

Bair also encourages teams to test out different survey cadences. Depending on your company's needs, that may mean trying pulse surveys, monthly questionnaires, or something completely different:

> We've made the decision to hold engagement surveys with different topics on a quarterly basis, and we're seeing pretty good engagement, . . . But we're always trying to see what we can do to change it up, to make sure that we're accurately capturing sentiment.

---

[3]Andy Przystanski, "How to Calculate Employee Net Promoter Score (eNPS)," Lattice website (April 14, 2020), https://lattice.com/library/what-is-employee-net-promoter-score-enps

How Surveys Become Action

Once the survey has been conducted and the results are in, it's time to develop an action plan. No matter how strong your company culture, there will always be room for improvement, and how you leverage that data from your people will show them you're committed to making those improvements. Once you've identified those areas that need change, the next step is to create actionable goals around those needed changes. Whatever goals you create around addressing an identified area of improvement, those goals should be specific, with a clear means and an end; they should be measurable, allowing you to track your progress clearly and the way in which it will be accomplished; they should be realistic, something that is relevant to your team, and that addresses factors that are under your control; and finally, they should be based on a clear timetable.

For instance, with more employees working from home as a result of the coronavirus pandemic, your survey may show that working from home has left employees feeling disconnected from the company culture. The circumstances that created the remote working situation might not be something you can control, but there are certainly measures that you can take to help those working virtually feel more included. Maybe you start holding company-sponsored happy hours over teleconference each month. It's a small fix, but one that could go a long way toward fostering the kind of camaraderie some newly remote employees might be missing while working virtually.

Once you decide on your plan of action, it's important to communicate it both to company leaders and employees at large. Doing so not only makes clear to employees that you are serious about their concerns, but it also provides accountability for managers tasked with implementing the measures. The goal of the plan is to take the survey and turn it into programs that can transform the culture.

Lattice's Pandemic Response Survey

Lattice had an opportunity to leverage our surveying expertise internally in order to sort out how our culture was being deeply affected by the pandemic. After roughly a month of all working from home, our People team rolled out an initial survey, asking about everything from whether folks had the right tools and equipment to whether they felt they were struggling morale-wise.

Soon after, Lattice's Vice President of People Dave Carhart started at the company, he rolled out a second survey to dig a bit deeper and develop more meaningful programs:

In that survey, we drilled in on three areas that were beyond the immediate crisis – what are the emotional or deeper needs of our people who are being affected by something that is really big and horrible and ongoing. Out of that, there were three particular areas that came out as the biggest concerns: stress, motivation, and connection.

First, we came up with a few good, quick actions. We committed to seriously working on promoting mental health. To improve motivation, we planned a meeting for managers to talk about and share information on how each is dealing with these challenges. We also came up with a shared page with a list of icebreakers as ideas for teams to use to improve connectedness.

Next, we rolled out a couple of more programmatic pieces, engaging managers a bit – promoting a benefit around mental health – to start to address those.

Then, rather than running another COVID survey, we said, "Okay well look, there are three questions there that we said were the concerns from last time." So, we followed up with shorter pulse surveys, and we found that motivation for people had actually substantially bounced back. Basically, I think we found that managers and teams were able to identify the sources of motivation, but I don't have a good way of explaining why.

Once we got past the initial or even the secondary crisis response, people's motivation returned, and people were really putting everything that they had into their jobs.

We found that stress was a little bit down. As an ongoing concern, we found that "connection" continued to fall. And that, for us, was the source of the really deep and ongoing pain.

So, what we're working on now is continuing to talk with managers, and reorienting our culture events strategy. Instead of creating more broad company Zoom meetups and happy hours, we focused on providing managers with a resource to facilitate social events easily, which are intended to deepen the relationships and social connections on their team, especially given all the people who joined during the pandemic. And we're working to develop the next phase as well, where we start to go beyond social events and roll out more team-based workshops.

So I think knowing where the real pain is found in the organization, not just at a point in time but on an ongoing basis, allows us to figure out both how to respond most effectively in the moment, and then how to make deeper and more substantial investments in the long-term programs that will truly support the culture over the next year.

Earlier, we talked about how monitoring performance requires not only the big annual review but more frequent, routine check-ins. The same holds true when we track progress toward engagement and company culture goals – regular communication and maintenance are required. It's vital for HR and managers of managers to set recurring one-on-one meetings with team managers to see how they are implementing the action plan and how employees seem to be responding. This one-on-one meeting can serve both as an opportunity for managers to update progress and to adjust goals as needed, perhaps by brainstorming alternative solutions if the current path is not getting the desired result.

Another important way of tracking progress is through the use of pulse surveys – short, 1–5 question surveys that are quick to complete and can be administered as needed to provide data in real time. These are quick checkups to gain immediate insights into engagement and allow employers to gauge the impact of their programs and to make informed business decisions. These hyper-focused surveys don't provide the holistic, big picture insights that engagement surveys do, but they can illuminate trends quickly and indicate whether or not your adjustments are making an impact.

In that same Lattice State of People Strategy Survey, on top of annual engagement surveys, over 50 percent of HR respondents said that they leverage limited engagement surveys (such as the COVID/crisis-response survey that ParkHub and Lattice used) and nearly 60 percent used pulse surveys to track progress between bigger surveys. These are proven tools in the standard people strategy toolbox.

By repeating this process over and over, you can ensure the vitality of your company culture. It's easy to fall into the trap of thinking that culture is something that comes about magically. But the reality is that creating a culture requires intent and constant maintenance. I learned that the hard way at Teespring, where I watched what had been a vibrant, supportive company culture grow toxic and unviable. When I created Lattice, I wanted above all else to make sure that the company was a place where people loved to work, felt connected and valued, and could grow – both as individuals and within the organization. We tried to weave our values of community, purpose, and growth into everything we did, and I believed we were successful.

But it wasn't until that culture was tested by the coronavirus pandemic that I knew for sure. The culture we'd tried so hard to cultivate and sustain showed up when it was most important. Our relationships were deepened, our sense of purpose was further clarified, and our values became something of a buoy that we could cling to in those challenging times. When we think of a strong company culture, we often think about the good times – how it can make the good times seem great and attract great employees and retain talent and increase productivity. But the pandemic underscored just how much a vibrant culture and engaged employees can bind a company together during some of its most challenging moments.

Engagement Survey Plan Checklist

So, you've run your engagement survey, now what? We just talked through the important steps for how to turn those results into action. Here's a quick summary checklist of all those steps:

1. **Analyze your results.** You don't need to be a data scientist to glean insights from your employees' responses.
    a. Look at both the demographic and organizational cross-sections of data.
    b. Read the comments and encourage department and team leaders to read the comments that are relevant for their areas.
    c. Compare historical data and benchmark results.

2. **Build your plan.** Once your data tells its story, you can take those insights, recommend how to act, get buy-in, and put a plan in place.

   a. Share your results with leadership.

   b. Identify priorities with managers.

   c. Set engagement goals.

   d. Share your plan with the company through an organization-wide, all-hands presentation and email.

3. **Track Progress.** Once you've built your action plan and targets, goal stakeholders will need to track progress and adjust as needed, and HR can help by providing them with updates along the way.

   a. Using pulse surveys is a great way to check in on progress of initiatives.

   b. Check in with managers and even employees by attending team meetings or setting up one-on-one time.

   c. Share your progress publicly through all-hands check-ins or company emails, and make sure to celebrate wins as you see anything greatly improve.

Key Points

- Culture benefits employees and companies alike.
- A strong company culture doesn't just crop up magically – it takes conscious effort to foster and maintain.
- Engagement surveys are the most effective way to take the temperature of a culture and identify areas that need work.
- There will always be room for improvement – developing a clear, measurable plan of action, and communicating that to employees is essential to troubleshooting.

5

Prioritizing Growth

Humans are wired for growth.

We are always seeking out new opportunities and challenges: looking to improve ourselves or our careers, taking on new responsibilities, and adapting and evolving as people and workers. We want to be happy in the moment, but we also want to look back on the long arcs of our lives and see ourselves building new things over the years. This is especially true in our fast-moving world in which skills have an ever-shorter shelf life, and the labor market remains uncertain. A recent survey conducted by consulting firm Guthrie-Jensen (https://guthriejensen.com/blog/statistics-employee-training/) found that three-quarters of American workers are looking for growth opportunities at work; even more Millennials say that they value development opportunities, with 87 percent of respondents saying that career growth is "very important."

Companies that recognize the importance of employee development are better positioned to attract and retain talent. According to the 2018 LinkedIn Workplace Learning Report (https://learning .linkedin.com/resources/workplace-learning-report-2018), 94 percent of employees would stay at a company longer if it presented them with sufficient growth and development opportunities. And a Zaki Warfel survey (https://courses.zakiwarfel.com/dci-report) found that companies that invest in leadership and career development see a 250 percent longer employee tenure.

And this fact isn't lost on most HR teams. In our State of People Strategy Survey, "Learning and Development" ranked fourth as a top-priority initiative for 2021, and 60 percent said that L&D was the number one program for which they wish they could get more support from their companies.

Employees, particularly Millennials, are intensely focused on what they can get from their employers, mostly when it comes to growth and learning opportunities. They are interested in furthering their careers and want to align with a company that makes that a priority. For companies concerned with retaining their best people and making them more productive, finding ways to help them further their careers – within and outside of the company – is essential.

Helping Employees Develop

Growth for employees can ensure growth for your business. If your people feel like you're investing in them, they'll invest double in your success. Of course, that can be easier said than done. For companies and managers, there hasn't always been clarity around what growth looks like – in part, because they've lacked clear infrastructure and processes to manage employee growth.

Heather Doshay, vice president of People at Webflow, a Lattice customer, explained it to us this way:

> Ultimately, there's two pieces to this puzzle of career development, and they're different. One is career development, and one is career advancement. Career development is how you grow skills, how it will make you successful in future roles. It's how you up-level yourself to be ready for the challenges that come ahead of you in the job that you're in, the job that you want to go to. Career advancement is a promotion, maybe higher pay. And most times people are thinking about career advancement. They're not thinking about career development.
>
> And what companies are often thinking about is, "How do we develop people so that they can be up-skilled and be eligible to do a certain job and do it well? And how do we build those skills within that person?" But [employees] are thinking about *advancement* – promotions, recognition that is monetary and title based, and potentially job scope based as well. Helping folks understand through really thoughtful structures is how you get both, and how development is just as meaningful for a career.

Career pathing provides that structure – it offers a clear look ahead for employees within a certain role, at a certain level. But while employee development is an essential function of human resources, that career-pathing exercise isn't always a part of employee development. On its face, it seems simple – a process by which an employee charts their development plan within the company to identify opportunities for which they might be a fit, based on their interests, experiences, and competencies. But in practice, there's a lot more to it. Successful career pathing is more than just managers asking their employees where they see themselves 5 or 10 years down the line. It should be a more assertive, proactive, and organized practice, moving toward a goal of establishing a kind of harmony, balancing what the company needs with what the employee needs.

A *career path* is a sequence of jobs an employee aims to hold throughout their time at an organization. It maps out potential roles and the skills, knowledge, competencies, experience, and personal characteristics required for each job level as an employee moves up the ladder.

"It's basically giving the team member a map to say, 'Hey, here's all the places you can go. You have to get yourself there. And our management team will help you,'" said Doshay. "Imagine the individual employee is driving the car in the metaphor. The manager is basically a backseat driver, helping them guide them as to where to go. And the company builds the map that helps the two navigate the process together."

While career paths traditionally go from entry level to executive level within a department, not all career growth is vertical. Career paths can be flexible and allow employees to move laterally or cross-functionally as well. (See Figure 5.1.) Having a detailed framework in place makes it easy for employees to understand which of their skills are transferable to other departments and roles within an organization, and it encourages internal career changes.

For employers, career pathing can help engage and retain talent because it shows people their growth opportunities within the organization. Career paths can help employees envision a long-term career at your company, increasing employee retention, and reducing hiring costs. It can also help you identify skills gaps in your current workforce, showing you where you need to train to grow talent within your company or where to make your next external hire.

Melissa Cadwallader, MBA, PHR, an HR leader at ZenBusiness, an Austin-based business formation service company, told us the following about career pathing:

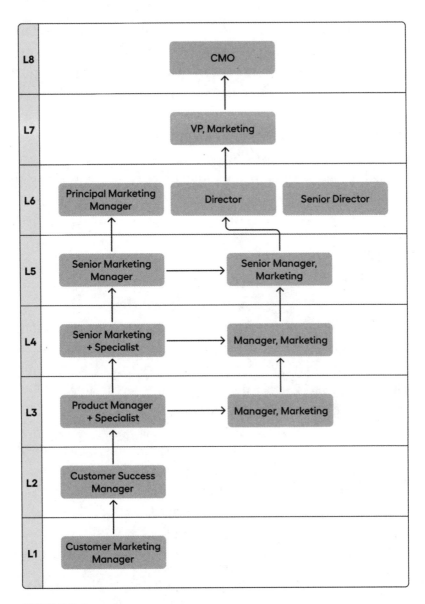

FIGURE 5.1

Investment in career pathing will also safeguard the business, as employees are equipped with the skills and knowledge required to move into senior positions . . . This process of workforce optimization will inevitably result in increased productivity and profitability.

The most apparent benefit for employees is understanding internal career opportunities and using this information to establish long-term and short-term career goals. This can motivate them to do their best work, take on different challenges, and learn new skills.

Plus, it's also reassuring as an employee to know that your company is invested in your career growth. This sense of direction enables employees to set and achieve milestones along the way and ultimately get closer to achieving their career goals.

The Growth Mistakes of High Growth

Heather Doshay, vice president of People at Webflow, has spent much of her career helping high-growth tech start-ups in the Silicon Valley to develop their HR teams and right the wrongs that often happen in the early years of a start-up's life.

I'll give you a story of how start-ups generally run: The CEO decides he's going to found a company, a software company, with a different technical cofounder. They build this initial product. They have no money, so they can't really hire the best talent. They have ambiguous jobs and do more than one thing, because they only hire five people.

They hire generalists who are relatively inexperienced because that's who they can afford. They hire, let's call the person, Sam. Sam is the CEO's friend who lives down the street. Sam could probably do the job and is willing to accept very little money. Sam's like, "Cool. I've never done this job before. I'll figure it out. I'm so resourceful. I'm a generalist."

Two years down the road, now they're a company of 50. They need to hire five more people that do what Sam does. So, they say, "Sam, you know this stuff better than anybody. We're going to make you a manager. Go hire a team." But (1) Sam doesn't have a clear understanding of what it looks like to be good at that job, (2) Sam does not have any experience of doing the job that they're in, let alone the job that they're going to advance to, and (3) being a manager of a team is very different than his existing job. And it's positioned as management is the path to promotion.

This is when you need to set expectations for advancement – policies or procedures for how do we get from here to there. And if you're a CEO of a start-up, policies and procedures are four-letter words. You don't want your people to feel restricted; you want them to be creative. All of these structured things feel very picky and very counterintuitive to a start-up CEO.

But as companies scale quickly, they'll realize that that person that they hired when they were 20 people, isn't truly executive. They might be professional, and this might be their opportunity as a professional to advance to a different role in their future.

People hired as "head of" a department are thinking, "Oh, well, if I can be 'head of,' this is my fast track to executive." Later, the CEO realizes, "Shoot, we really need a true VP of Marketing. We need someone who can scale this team. This head of Marketing isn't working out well." Now you tell this "head of" person what they're really leveled as, and you have to go backward and find out where they fit in this map.

Now, five years down the road, they end up in this predicament that the person they hired to do X job is now the manager of a growing team who's completely under-qualified for that role. And they wonder why they're behind.

Avoiding doing that at all costs can be so, so huge. And really helping build these processes early can help. Establish very clear frameworks for what it means to operate at every level and every role across your company's universe.

The number one reason why people leave companies is not based on compensation. Depending on which survey you pull, it's either a bad manager, which is all the folks that work under the person you just promoted who doesn't know what they're doing, or it's, "I don't see a future for myself here. I don't see myself aligned with the company's priorities and goals. I don't know why I'm here."

That's what happens when there's no company infrastructure, no job description, no clear career pathways for what it means to operate at this level versus that level.

Daniel Kahneman wrote the book *Thinking, Fast and Slow* (Farrar, Straus and Giroux, 2013) about Type One thinking, which is fast, and Type Two, which is slow and deliberate. A lot of times when we're hiring people quickly in start-ups and we're making promotion decisions, we're going on gut instinct. We're relying on our biases. We're not thinking deeply because we have so many other big, scary decisions to make as CEOs of businesses. But you're promoting people who don't have the skills you need, and who won't scale up the organization.

When you're using Type One decision making, you end up missing thing, and nobody has time to use Type Two decision making on a promotion. So what I advocate for is spending a little bit of time investing in either hiring your first People person, hire a consultant who can build this for you, or buying a product like Lattice that has the system set up. Then you don't have to waste time thinking about every individual decision around upscaling your promotion as this very deep thought process.

It's important that you have something that's structured, that is going to evolve over time. The thing you create when you're 50 people is not going to work when you're 2,000 people. But you've got some time between 50 to 2,000 to innovate and to iterate on those processes. And to learn with a small group of 50 is much easier to see what works and doesn't work about your process than when your 2,000 and rolling out across a global team.

Creating a Growth Framework

The first step in setting up career pathing as a practice is setting up the pathways, and defining pathways comes through a competency matrix. Competency matrices will serve as the backbone of talent planning across teams within your organization. Once set up, you can see which people are needed for different functions at your company, what junior to senior level roles look like in those functions, and what it means to be great at those roles. A matrix will create clear guidelines and a shared language for roles across the company and will help inform who you need to hire, who you need to train, and even how they should be paid.

It never ceases to amaze me that most companies don't have a system like this in place at all (which was a big reason for us to create Grow as a product at Lattice). Many companies think they're too small or too young or maybe even think that it's just not that necessary. But we would argue that, even if rolled out in as lightweight a way as possible, such a system can help employees envision their growth and also help HR and the company to plan effectively.

"Some of the reasons why people don't implement these things is because they see it and the alarm bells go off as like, 'This is structure and process that's clunky and not necessary!'" Anabel Lippincott Paksoy of HR consultancy The People Design House told me. "But [when we advise start-up founders], we do spend a ton of time making the case of why it's always necessary and foundational."

Doshay separately adds that it's not just process for process sake:

> If you think about it this way, a job architecture is this entire system and structure of organizing the entire universe of jobs [that] exist in your company. It's a system that will help you scale your entire business and will share understanding of what it means to be successful at every stage in your career. It's great for the HR leaders who will build systems around it. It's great for the individual [employees] to see what's expected. It's great for new managers looking to set expectations. It's great for the leader to have a scalable process over time.

> Building out those frameworks in advance – one, helps you as a company evaluate your talent better; two, helps [employees] understand where they're at and helps set expectations; and three, for HR, those levels could serve as the foundation for compensation bands, for promotion choices, and more.

So how do you begin? A basic matrix consists of two parts: competencies and levels.

Competencies are the skills or characteristics needed to succeed in a role, regardless of how junior or senior the employees in that track might be.

Job levels indicate the range of positions that exist along a track, and contain differentiated expectations around each competency for each level, from most junior to most senior.

Job Competencies

The competencies part of a matrix for a job function or family (such as Marketing or Engineering or Human Resources) should be consistent across the family, regardless of experience. These are the basic areas that you want the business to fulfill at the end of the day, and you need to define those areas before you start breaking out layers of roles.

We worked with Anabel Lippincott Paksoy and her partner Nathalie McGrath from The People Design House to design competencies for our Grow customer template. To start, we agreed that competencies need to be observable and objective:

> **Observable:** Because your managers and leaders will need to identify whether an employee is embodying and exhibiting those competencies.
>
> **Objective:** Because different people will inevitably have different standards and definitions, and one of the main advantages of having competency matrices is the ability to have a level playing field for all employees.

Next, when developing the competencies for different families, they recommend looking at a function within the organization and thinking about these four themes:

> **Impact (or "what the job is"):** This is the impact that the individuals in this function have on the product, the company, and even on the market.
>
> **Behaviors (or "how the job gets done"):** These are the specific behaviors, such as collaboration and communication, that help this team support the company and its values.
>
> **Management (or "the people management work that the role requires"):** What does it mean to be an effective manager

at this company? These spell out the characteristics of great managers and translate them into measurable behaviors.

Functional skills (or "what skills and experience are necessary to do the role"): These get into the specific skills and knowledge needed for success within this function.

Keep in mind that competencies are distinctly different from OKRs or goals. One way to identify a competency versus a goal is to consider where it falls in the following two categories:

A. Longevity: Is it long-lasting (that is, a competency) or relevant for a given quarter or year (in other words, a goal)?

B. Universality: Is it universal for all individuals in a given role (that is, a competency) or only relevant for a specific individual or team (in other words, a goal)?

Speaking to us in 2020, Julie Jensen, principal at Moxie HR Strategies, who has been helping organizations write job competencies for 20 years, recommended dividing competencies into two categories – company-wide and role-specific.

This is similar to how Todd Zaki Warfel, of ZW & Co, encourages his clients to build their matrices as well – for smaller companies that have more generalists, there may be more of an emphasis on company-wide competencies; as companies become more complex, you see more role-specific competencies emerge.

Company-wide competencies are, by their nature, broader in scope – a set of skills and expectations every member of the organization should embody, ideally informed by the company values we discussed in the earlier chapter on hiring. This is similar to the "impact" and "behaviors" part of the Lattice approach.

Role-specific competencies, meanwhile, are narrower – the expectations that each job and job level carry with them. This is close to the "functional skills" area from earlier. Jensen told us:

Clearly defining and describing each level of competency is helpful for managers and employees to fully understand what it is that's being asked of them. It also helps take much of the subjectivity away when definitions contain tangible examples.[1]

Job Levels

Once you've written out those competencies, you'll next take on *job leveling*, or *job classification* – a process that human resources leaders use to define the actual "levels" of a job track, develop career pathways and internal mobility processes, and create clear job hierarchies within an organization. Much in the same way that clear expectations are essential to evaluating employee performance, job leveling ensures that employees know precisely what is expected of them – both in the jobs they are in today and the jobs that they hope to be in in the future. If the process is effective, it can help your company foster an environment in which employees are successful, their needs and those of the organization are met, and the workplace is more equitable.

As a report from Deloitte put it, job leveling should provide:

A sound, easy-to-use system for determining the value of jobs based on talent drivers, business needs, and market practices . . . consistent methodology and decision support for assigning job levels and titles that are based on enterprise-wide criteria, which eliminates guesswork and promotes trust and confidence in the organization's job assignments and rewards practices" and establishes "workforce planning and career paths that are logical, transparent, fiscally responsible, and support employees and strategic business needs.[2]

---

[1]Andy Przystanski, "What Are Job Competencies and Why Do They Matter?," Lattice website (June 17, 2020), https://lattice.com/library/what-are-job-competencies-and-why-do-they-matter

[2]Steve Chanthadavong, Rachel Ferber, and Christine Robovsky, "Job Architecture: Laying the Building Blocks of Effective Human Capital Management," Deloitte website (2015), p. 1, https://www2.deloitte.com/content/dam/Deloitte/us/Documents/human-capital/us-cons-job-architecture-041315.pdf

Every company will have a slightly different approach to job leveling because, naturally, every company is different and has its own unique set of needs. If you're a start-up, your company might have fewer job levels and a less strict hierarchical structure. Employees might wear many different hats, the structure might be flatter, and responsibilities might be shared across several departments. But at a company like, say, Microsoft, job leveling would be vastly different; there will be many levels, a much clearer hierarchy within the company, and a far more obvious delineation between roles and responsibilities.

Our partners at The People Design House helped us set up the Lattice template with universalizable job levels that contain both a number ("Level 1," "Level 2," and so on) as well as a general title ("Associate," "Developing," "Professional," and so on). As we discussed earlier, each level should spell out the expectations around each competency, depending on where an individual is along a track. The track shows the role's progression – starting from the least sophisticated expression of those competencies at the junior level to the most sophisticated expression at the senior levels. As employees master competencies at the junior level, a manager can then move them up the track by giving them more responsibility and ownership generally marked by a promotion.

In June 2020, we spoke to Sarah Dabby, the head of People for the timesheet platform ClickTime (https://www.clicktime .com/), who made a point about leveling that resonated with me. She said that regardless of size, all companies should always consider four key components when thinking about job leveling: pay, purpose, progress, and people. And each of those components should answer a very specific question.

Pay: Am I not only compensated fairly but in a way that meets individual needs?

Purpose: Do I know why I'm showing up?

Progress: Do I know what I'm making strides toward in the workplace, and that I'm developing new skills?

People: Do I enjoy being around and working with my colleagues as much as I enjoy my job?

Additionally, it is important to make sure that your job leveling framework is easy to use and explain both to managers and their reports. If one of the aims here is to ensure that everyone has a clear understanding of what is expected of them, those expectations must be easy to communicate. After all, a vast majority of American workers say that they are in the dark when it comes to career growth; in a 2019 survey by the Harris Poll for Infrastructure (https:// www.businessnewsdaily.com/15085-disconnect-employee -development.html), 77 percent of respondents said they "feel like they're on their own" when it comes to development. If your job leveling framework isn't helping employees feel that they are supported in their career journey and that there is a clear path at your company to reaching their goals, then it isn't working.

One issue to consider when building out levels is the difference between individual contributors and managers. An *Individual Contributor (IC)* is someone without management responsibilities and who is generally more tactical within a team. *Managers* are more strategic, overseeing a team and a team's priorities and responsibilities. Most importantly, managers own the development of a team and steering that team toward accomplishing team goals.

As ICs consider advancing their careers, they may think the best logical next step to better pay and a promotion is by aiming to become a manager. But that's not always the best next step. Webflow's Heather Doshay explains why:

> An IC's job is not a step below a manager. Promoting to a manager is a whole different job path that runs parallel and is a unique

skillset itself. And it's a very unique place to be a people manager coming from an IC role because you're doing a different job.

Developing IC and manager tracks separately, each with more seniority and with robust competency descriptions, could help ease those conversations if an IC's manager is trying to help them determine the right next step. Doshay continues:

> It's important to think about how you build a system that rewards and recognizes individual contributors specifically, so that they're seen as a role to be desired as opposed to the waiting space into the management.

Job leveling matrices can provide that needed clarity. By combining job levels with competencies in one view, HR teams and managers give their people clarity on the road ahead. Job levels are the roles, responsibilities, and salaries that make up a company's hierarchy.

Job competencies are the skills or qualities that an employee needs to succeed in their given role. For instance, an entry-level product manager might have among their core competencies and abilities to articulate clearly what a product does and why. The second level communication competency would include an ability to seek feedback, synthesize information, and articulate that up the ladder. The senior-level communication competency would feature an ability to discuss context and feedback with stakeholders, both external and internal, and to communicate those back at scale.

Each new job level comes with new, clearly articulated competencies that allow the company to show an employee what level they are at and what they need in order to get where they want to go, standardizing and making the promotion process fairer. Alongside OKRs, competencies set expectations for employees and give them a path forward and upward, showing where they are now and where they can go next, as well as what they need to do in their role to get there.

Competencies and levels are particularly valuable for managers, as they can serve as a reference point when giving feedback, writing performance reviews, or delegating tasks. They can also help your team customize internal training, as well as recruit staff. Additionally, competencies can help identify skill gaps more efficiently.

Doshay likes to point out that companies collecting this information from managers can help them gain real clarity in talent management overall.

> You can ask for the right development opportunities and figure out where the skill gaps are across the company. Using a tool like this, you can audit where are we weak as a business, where are we strong? How can we build trainings and outsource opportunities for folks? How can we decide when it's time to bring another VP in? What will we actually get if we brought on a VP in this function versus keeping the senior managers that we have? It just allows you to have more clarity into the whole picture by building up those systems.

Together, job levels and competencies help clarify where the employee is in their development, what the next level up will be, and what is needed to get there. They help define what success looks like, making it easier for managers to establish expectations and set a bar for performance. They illuminate the pathway for a particular role, helping managers and employees determine if they are right for a role and where they want to be down the line – and, if a particular role is not working out, they can help determine a path that may be a better fit for employees looking to switch directions.

How to Get Started Writing Competencies and Levels

In helping design the competencies template for our Grow product in Lattice, The People Design House wanted to write them in a way that made it easy for any company to have a starting point. We identified universal competencies that could apply to most roles, and also left room for HR leaders and managers to fill in company- and role-specific details as well.

If you're just getting started, use our template to begin writing your own. But note that no matter how universal the starter set may be, we encourage you to adjust them according to what's true for your company's culture and needs.

Competencies:

- Start with the role: Are you defining competencies for Sales? Marketing? Customer Care?
- Remember our areas of definition:

Impact: Why does the company need this role?

Behaviors: What behaviors will help this role work successfully within the company?

Management: What characteristics will make leaders in this role successful?

Functional skills: What skills are specific to this role? These could vary from level to level.

Here are some examples of poorly defined competencies, why they don't work, and how to make them better:

Poorly defined competency	Why this isn't useful	Instead try . . .
You are trustworthy and get things done. You are active in the company and people like you.	• Not observable • Lacks specificity as to what it means to be "trustworthy" and to "get things done." • "People like you" is subjective and not able to be effectively observed.	You **do what you say you're going to do** or **communicate promptly** to set **expectations** appropriately. You **rarely** miss work, but you quickly follow through when reminded.
You don't take no for an answer, and you know how to push to get things done.	• Not inclusive or objective. • Describes a personality versus identifying an expected output. • Places a value judgment on a certain approach to accomplishing a goal.	You effectively **address and resolve basic conflicts** with **function and company.** You **proactively engage in productive dialog even when there are conflicting views**, both inside and outside the team.
You take responsibility for our holiday order fulfillment process design, driving it to completion with minimal supervision.	• Not durable or long-lasting. This describes a goal versus a repeatable behavior or characteristic.	You **consistently** deliver **and actively** help others deliver on work. You are accountable for the reliability of your project, group, function, etc.

Job levels:

Here's a sample matrix universalized leveling template, breaking employee development up across both the IC and manager tracks:

Level	Job level 1	Job level 2	Job level 3	Job level 4	Job level 5	Job level 6
IC Career Stage	Associate	Developing	Professional	Senior Professional	Expert	Principal
Manager Career Stage	-	-	Manager	Senior Manager	Director	VP
Notes on this stage	These are entry levels and employees often progress through these more quickly. It's uncommon for employees to stay within these job levels throughout their careers. Typically, there are no management roles at these levels.		It's common for a successful career-level professional to reach these job levels and remain here for the entirety of their career. This is not considered stagnating as a majority of critical work is accomplished within these job levels. People management most commonly starts at Job Level 3.		These are positions that are commonly reached after deep functional and/or professional experience. Moving into and between these job levels is often slower as the roles increase significantly in complexity and seniority. It is common for people managers at these levels to have other managers as direct reports.	

Fill each state and level using your competencies, showing progression.

Remember, level the role, not the person. Don't make these personalized to any employee, or they won't be objective. Create levels and assign expectations to each track without focusing on any person who currently fills that role. Once the track has been leveled, then assign that right level to the person or people in the role.

Developing a Growth Plan

All of this can help your organization develop growth plans for your employees. Not to be confused with a performance improvement plan, this is a road map that sits alongside goals and establishes a personal development plan for an employee. Goals and OKRs are a set-time framework for helping an employee see how their work helps the business move forward by laddering what they work on up to the goals for the company overall. A growth plan, meanwhile, is a set-time framework that shows the employee how their work helps *them progress personally* in their career, both within and outside of their particular responsibilities for the company. While well-defined job tracks allow employees to see what pathways are available to them within the organization, growth plans allow them to build their own, unique path through those tracks, or outside of them. Indeed, an effective growth plan should also allow employees to see a path forward in their next job, at their next company, and beyond. If goals, OKRs, and other performance management frameworks are focused more on what the company needs, growth plans are mainly concerned with what the employee needs – a crucial element of People Strategy.

A growth plan can help employees take their career to the next level, helping them cultivate and hone skills and proficiencies that can help them develop within their current roles, progress within the company, and prepare for opportunities beyond. While these plans can reference the competencies of job levels on a given job track, they aren't necessarily tied to specific tasks and expectations, like sales quotas or sales leads. An effective professional development plan is designed to bolster competencies that enhance an employee's value. Some companies take a hands-on approach to employee growth, providing development programs within the organization. Others leave personal professional development up to employees, providing development stipends that can be used at the discretion of each individual. Some take a hybrid approach.

There are some key considerations when establishing growth plans.

The first is to help employees set clear, achievable targets. What are the skills they would like to obtain or improve upon? What are some of the characteristics, aptitudes, and proficiencies they need to move to the next level of their career? What existing strengths does the employee have that they can leverage to be even more competitive in their career going forward? These are some of the questions to weigh in developing a growth plan.

"Ultimately, when considering the map analogy, you could have a car, you could have a map, but you're not going to get to where you're going without some gasoline – the knowledge, the tools, and resources to drive the car," said Doshay about the next step in executing a plan. "There's always going to be a gap between where somebody is on the map, and where they want to go on that map. And even though you provided this map on where what's needed, what skills are missing, what gaps are there that are needing to be developed in order to get there, how do folks develop those skills?"

A good way to answer those questions can be to look at those who are already succeeding in a given role. Ephraim Schachter, president of the performance management consultancy Schachter Consulting (https://www.schacterconsulting.com/), used the example of a prospective marketing director when he outlined his view of helping employees achieve professional development goals in 2020.

> Look at their career paths and the organizations they belong to and look at the commonalities . . . If five out of six marketing directors attend a certain conference, then attend that conference. If they have spent time developing their design skills, then sign up for a design skills class.[3]

The point is not necessarily to mimic someone else's career path; there are many avenues that may lead to a similar goal. But showing employees what others have done can help clarify their own direction.

Schachter continues:

> This doesn't have to be mysterious . . . There are other people already succeeding in what you want to do that you can emulate.

Managers should help support their employees' growth – both as professionals and as people – through productive development conversations. These discussions show your team

---

[3]Jennifer Ernst Beaudry, "4 Steps for Setting (and Achieving) Professional Development Goals," Lattice website (June 11, 2020), https://lattice.com/library/4-simple-steps-for-setting-and-achieving-professional-development-goals

members that you're invested in them beyond their daily tasks, as well as highlight what they need to feel fulfilled and engaged at work. This benefits the employee, as well as the company, which will be able to better retain and grow talent while potentially developing talent internally to move up from within. Effective conversations should be employee-led, allowing employees to define their aspirations and measures of success. And for these conversations, growth plans should also be the sole agenda item, making clear to employees that their personal growth is valued by the company and not merely an afterthought to be tagged on to a performance review or some other meeting.

Steer employees toward the concrete, ensuring that both the employee and the manager leaves with clear next steps to pursue to help the employee realize their goals. "Development is not just about a promotion or the next position," LaShawn Davis, founder of the HR Plug (https://www.thehrplug.com/), a company that provides HR services to employers and employees alike. She continued:

It's about stretching the abilities and talents employees have. It's about challenging them to think differently, take bold risks, and develop themselves, which by default will bring value to the organization. It's about reminding them who they are, what they bring, and what they can accomplish, and coaching them to produce and strengthen and develop those skills.[4]

By having these conversations regularly, you can not only help develop and support your employees' growth plans, but you can also hold them accountable to the goals they have set.

[4]Deanna deBara, "How to Have Successful Employee Development Conversations," Lattice website (June 25, 2020), https://lattice.com/library/how-to-have-successful-employee-development-conversations

Looking Beyond Growth Plans

Of course, growth plans are not the only ways HR teams and managers can support employee development; they're really just the start. While growth plans help employees see where they want to grow next professionally and the skills or experience, they need to get there, now employees – with the support of their managers and companies – can actually begin developing.

"Ultimately, with career development, it's a chance to really invest in the person as a way to have very clear expectations around what skills can be grown and added in order to develop into that next level and get that career advancement," explained Doshay. "And then what ends up happening when you do all of this is that people can really scale with an organization."

There are many learning and development (L&D) programs that employers, HR professionals, and managers can put in place to show employees that the company is invested in their development and helping them achieve their professional goals.

One important way to help employees develop is through training. Traditionally, the idea of training has focused on the 70-20-10 model, in which 70 percent of learning occurs on the job; 20 percent comes from others, and 10 percent comes through courses and other more formal avenues. (https://www.ccl.org/articles/leading-effectively-articles/70-20-10-rule/)

Doshay explained:

This is a really common percentage map that's thought about in the L&D community, in the learning and development community. . . 70% is experiential – new and challenging experiences, on the job experiences. That's where people are really getting the bulk of their learning at companies. It's not happening in a formal classroom and learning. Most of what you've learned is from applicable on-the-job experiences that have stretched you and helped you grow. So really, what it's about is managers using these gaps to find projects, opportunities, and various areas of the business that they can really stretch and grow into that help them get to that next level. And career pathways are helpful with that, too.

Managers should dig into the growth plan with their reports. Are there duties that a manager can delegate to give their employee a new experience to own or lead a project? Can they partner with someone within the company who has deep experience in a skill new to them that the manager can help enable? Doshay continued:

> And, 10 percent is happening in a classroom or program. If you're giving people opportunities to formally go to a training program where they can really study and learn and grow, all of those pieces certainly can be the cherry on top.

> And then lastly, there is social learning, which I actually would argue, for me at least, this is much more than 20 percent of my learning. This is joining communities, networks, coaching, mentoring, all those kinds of pieces that will help you grow and learn. And ultimately, these two pieces are more formalized, structured things that really.

Another potentially simple but important way to foster employee development is through coaching and mentoring.

Coaching goes beyond managing employees, which is geared more toward unilateral problem solving and directives. Where a manager may first lead with their personal expertise, advice, and direction, a *coach* is a performance-driven but explorational relationship. A coach may be someone hired on for their expertise to meet a specific development need.

Mentoring is more broadly focused on the longer arc of the employee's career, and productive mentoring relationships can go on for multiple years. Usually, a *mentor* is a more experienced person in the employee's current field who can be a confidante and adviser.

There's a time and place for both approaches. It may be worth exploring providing these services to employees. Some companies offer L&D stipends to spend on training or coaching programs. And often companies host mentoring programs internally, pairing up less experienced employees with more senior leaders.

Either way, taking a more coaching or mentoring approach with employees when it comes to development can help develop new skills and broaden their growth. Doshay advised, "Learning from peers, learning from more experienced people in the same field, informational interviews, . . . those pieces are all huge."

Such opportunities could become even more vital as companies embrace remote work. While companies should work to ensure that organizational culture remains strong, even if employees aren't coming into a physical office every day, the reality is that virtual-first companies can sometimes give short shrift to development. The 70-20-10 framework, in which a huge chunk of learning is to come from interactions with colleagues, may not be as effective when employees have fewer opportunities to directly interact. Without adequate access to training and other development programs, remote employees might miss out on needed opportunities to aid in their professional growth.

"When you think about why people leave companies, they don't see a future at their company," warned Doshay. "When you have this, you have painted out a future for them of where they could go within a broader map."

That's bad news, both for employees and for companies. As that 2018 LinkedIn Workplace Learning Report found, 94 percent of employees say that they're more likely to remain at their company if it presents opportunities for professional development. A 2016 Gallup poll found that 87 percent of Millennials view professional development or career growth opportunities as very important to them, suggesting that development opportunities not only helps companies grow their people, they help retain them. (https://www.gallup.com/workplace/236477/millennials-work-life.aspx)

Key Points

- Companies that recognize the importance of employee development are better positioned to attract and retain talent.

- Well-maintained job tracks provide a clear look ahead for employees, particularly those who crave structure.

- Competency matrices serve as the backbone of talent planning across teams within an organization.

- Growth plans enable employees to progress personally in their career, both within and outside of their particular responsibilities for the company.

CHAPTER

6

Leveraging Data

For most teams, data is a vital tool to drive business decisions. Sales teams, engineering teams, marketing teams – all of them use data to set goals, measure success, and inform strategy. But historically, human resources teams have not had that. Decisions about hiring and firing, promotions and performance management plans, and a host of other issues that face HR professionals have too often relied on judgment calls rather than hard numbers.

To some extent, this is unavoidable. When your work centers around human beings and human behavior, there will always be some subjectivity involved. But without quantitative measures, decision-making processes can feel shaky and lack transparency. And that can make it difficult for HR departments to position themselves as strategic to company leaders.

A significant aspect of any People Strategy requires observable and observed data to drive your decisions. Judgment is undoubtedly important, but we should never rely only on our gut. As a CEO, I want all my department leads to be able to present proof for their strategic plans and proof of results. HR is no exception. It's easy to think of People Strategy as a feel-good approach to HR, aimed only at ensuring that employees are happy. But through data and analytics, People Strategy also drives business outcomes – sometimes in unexpected ways.

Take this story that Courtney Cherry Ellis, vice president of human resources at Anaplan, told me recently. In a previous job, her company had dual offices in San Francisco and Washington, D.C. Seeking to learn more about retention, she and her colleagues dug into the data, performing regressions around compensation and other factors that one might assume played a role in keeping or losing employees. But what she found was that the biggest influence on tenure at the company was location. In Washington, D.C., employees tended to stay longer. But in San Francisco, where there was a greater abundance of opportunities and talent, employees tended to move around more. "Location wasn't necessarily something that we expected to see show up in that way," she recalled. "But we used that to really shift our location strategy."

Data can act as a "smoke signal" to show you where the fire is in your organization. It may not give you the exact terrain or tell you if the fires are spreading or not, but data provides you small-to-large indicators that then allow your HR team or company to follow up or build out new or better programs and focus. You can see surprising things in the data which lead you to go further and investigate through human interaction.

At Lattice, we had a manager once who seemed to be performing really well. He was recruiting effectively. He communicated well. He was smart, thoughtful, and doing great. At least it seemed he was until we ran an engagement survey.

This manager, we found, had some of the lowest engagement scores at the company. His direct reports were extremely
unhappy. They didn't feel supported by the manager. They didn't
feel as though they were getting good feedback. Just about on
every dimension of engagement, this team's results were low.

This, of course, came as a major surprise for us. We never
would have known that there was an issue. But the engagement
survey opened our eyes to something we weren't seeing before
and allowed us to dig a little deeper.

When we discussed the poor engagement metrics with this
manager, we found that he was as surprised as we were. As it
turns out, we shared the same blind spot. He was upset to learn
about these gaps in his performance, but he was open-minded to
the feedback and eager to course-correct. He resolved to devote
more time to his team and to work on his management skills and
was able to close those gaps. In alerting us and the manager to
an issue none of us knew existed, these "smoke signals" ended up
helping everyone: the manager, the employees, and the company.

Lattice began as a performance management company. But
in 2018, we had an "aha" moment, realizing that combining
performance management with employee engagement surveys
could yield better insights that, at the time, were missing from
HR. With these tools, we had the capacity not only to show if the
company culture was working for employees more broadly, but
we could also dig down and show how engaged top performers
are compared with bottom performers. Are high performers in
danger of leaving? Are some teams feeling less connected to the
organizational culture than others? And is that impacting their
productivity?

I knew these were the kinds of insights I wanted to see as
a CEO myself. We knew that there was a tremendous value in
pulling all of these different insights together under a single analytics tool, changing the way HR teams collect and analyze data,

and helping to arm them with the data they need to warrant a seat at the strategic table.

Data has become a more and more critical part of HR in recent years. As Lars Schmidt and David Green wrote in Fast Company in 2019, "People analytics offers enormous potential to organizations to drive business strategy, improve performance, and personalize and enhance the employee experience."[1] And studies back that up. Recent research by Visier found that better people analytics significantly benefit organizations (https://hello.visier.com/age-of-people-analytics-research-report/). So, perhaps it's no surprise that a 2019 myHRfuture report (https://tinyurl.com/yyqbxkwn) found that people analytics was the most sought-after skill among HR professionals; the benefit for companies is immense. Gallup noted in a 2017 report: "Powerful discoveries . . . make all the difference because they reveal outcome-driving actions . . . They help leaders translate raw data into improved operational effectiveness."[2]

This need to make HR more data-driven has been the biggest reason for the rise of HR technology like Lattice. For years, HR had to run critical data-gathering processes in text documents or spreadsheets. But HR technology has changed the way we can collect and analyze the data that drives many essential initiatives – from employee engagement to travel and expense management to rewards and recognition. When your HR tech stack is optimized to work together or centralizes a number of key data points under one tool, you can easily collect and even cross-reference data points to draw valuable insights to empower your team, even if you're not a data wonk.

---

[1]Lars Schmidt and David Green, "This Is Why Data Is Now More Essential Than Ever in HR," *Fast Company* (May 31, 2019), https://www.fastcompany.com/90357244/this-is-why-data-is-now-more-essential-than-ever-in-hr
[2]Ed O'Boyle, "How HR Leaders Can Win a Seat at the Table," *Gallup Workplace* (Dec 13, 2017), https://www.gallup.com/workplace/231644/leaders-win-seat-table.aspx

Moving Away from a "One Size Fits All" Approach

Courtney Cherry Ellis, vice president of human resources at Anaplan, knows that there's no "one size fits all" approach that works for every company. For a strategy to be effective, it must be tailored to a company's specific goals and aims. To drive that home, she related this example from the compensation space:

> There was for a time (and it still continues) a perspective that engineers were the group within your business for which you should be leveraging a different market pay-based approach. So, you would hear all these high-tech companies say, "We pay our people at the 50th percentile of market, with the exception of engineers, who we pay at the 75th percentile based on a salary survey." And that [practice] is because of scarcity of talent, the exceptionality, and the desire that they make or break a business . . . And that probably was anchored in a lot of the practices . . . that you saw at Google and Netflix.
>
> Now, I built my tech career at B2B fast companies. I will say, engineers . . . are incredibly important. So many of our employees are very important. But in a fast company, subscription revenue is your most important element. And that really is based not only on sales, but on customer retention. What might make sense for us is that our customer success team needs to be that exceptional superstar team, whether or not you pay them in a different way is based on internal strategy and philosophy.
>
> But there are a lot of business leaders who probably wouldn't listen to me if I were making the argument that your most

differentiated paid people need to be your customer success team, because that's not what the data says or that's not what best practice and industry standard is. But, in fact, that's what makes sense for your business and your business strategy is 100 percent dependent on retaining customers. And I think that's how your people strategy has to be intrinsically linked to your business strategy.

How to Leverage Data

Data is the key to proving that HR is a critical strategic function rather than a cost center that companies feel compelled to have. It shows what HR is capable of providing for an organization, just as marketing data demonstrates the value of the team and its strategy. It's how HR can translate people strategy into the executive language of numbers. But what data should you be analyzing?

It depends.

Because every company is different, HR teams are likely to have different needs and therefore different goals. Establishing what your goals are, then, is essential to understanding your analytics needs.

There are dozens of metrics that you could measure, but they all fall into a handful of categories. HR tracks all kinds of stats, but for the purposes of our people strategy discussion, we'll stick with the following:

Recruitment   Measuring the effectiveness and efficiency of your hiring funnel. *Examples: Time to hire and acceptance rate.*

Performance   Measuring how well employees and managers are performing against goals and expectation as well as how much employees are contributing to the business. *Examples: Goal tracking, performance review scores, and revenue per employee.*

Engagement   Measuring the health of your culture based on how many employees are staying and leaving, how many would recommend your company as a great place to work, and more. *Examples: eNPS, results from employee engagement surveys and pulse surveys, and turnover.*

Employee Development   Measuring the effectiveness and amount of learning and development happening at your company, including the number of employees who have received training, career pathing participation, as well as effectiveness of training efforts. *Examples: Training completion rate, career path ratio, and growth planning participation rate.*

Diversity, Equity, and Inclusion   For the purposes of tracking this very important category, HR leaders can encourage employees to voluntarily share their gender, preferred pronouns, and ethnicity information. HR can then generate transparent reporting on how diverse their company's workforce is in order to set goals. Also, HR can leverage compensation info in order to present a more transparent equitable pay report.

When we asked 570 HR professionals in our State of People Strategy Survey which "key performance indicators" or metrics matter most to them, a majority said that employee productivity, employee engagement, performance reviews, and voluntary turnover were the most important KPIs to measure the success of their HR teams.

Most of these KPIs actually include a group of metrics. "Employee productivity" could be one or all of the following:

Revenue by Employee, Output per Unit of Input, or even Turn-around Time; while "Performance Reviews" and "Employee Engagement" map to the Performance and Engagement categories.

As you get started mapping out those needs, remember this: most "people" metrics are not the sole responsibility of People teams. So, when setting expectations around the data piece of your People Strategy, keep in mind that there are really two types of metrics: organizational health metrics and People team metrics.

Organizational health metrics track how well employees are managed and are able to work within the company. HR may be on the hook to track and measure these metrics for the company, but these aren't usually numbers that HR can directly control or on which HR can move the needle without the participation of others in the organization. For example, employee engagement scores are measured and tracked as an HR responsibility, and HR programs can help improve engagement, but engagement is a company-wide effort – from the CEO to team leads to managers. HR programs alone won't make a real difference in lifting engagement overall.

These metrics are often a problem for People teams in that they can put the team into a "blame the messenger" scenario. "By making them solely people metrics, it feels like it sends a subconscious message that the people team is responsible for them, however engagement metrics [2–3 questions that measure an employee's engagement] are actually a measurement of your leadership team," said Nathalie McGrath of The People Design House.

People-centric companies should view "organizational health" as importantly as they view sales growth, customer satisfaction, or burn rate, and that often needs to start with prioritization at the executive or even CEO level.

But then there are *People Team metrics*, which are numbers that you and your team can directly control and should absolutely own. And even if some of those metrics do rely on other teams to help improve, they are metrics HR teams will want to drive outright to success.

HR Metrics 101

If you're just getting started and deciding which metrics to track, it may be easy to get overwhelmed by the options. We've put together a good starter list of metrics to help you get your data needs rolling. For most of these, you'll want to see how these metrics progress over time, reviewing them on a monthly or annual basis, depending on the metric.

In Hiring – Average Time to Fill

Measure how fast your recruiting team and the roles' hiring managers are filling positions – from when the job is listed until the moment a candidate is hired.

Average time to fill = sum of all roles' time to fill ÷ total number of openings filled

In Hiring – Cost per Hire

If your company is high growth, you'll want to be efficient with how much you're spending on recruiting. This metric will help you stay on budget, and a low cost per hire result is bragworthy.

Cost per hire = sum of internal and external hiring costs ÷ total hires in a given period

In Engagement – Employee Net Promoter Score (eNPS)

If you can't run a full-scale employee engagement survey, eNPS is an effective overall measure of employee engagement. It asks the simple question: *On a scale of 0 to 10, how likely are you to recommend your company as a place to work?* Employees with 9+ ratings are generally considered "promoters," while those with ratings of 0–6 and 7–8 are labeled as detractors and passive, respectively.

eNPS = % promoters – % detractors

An eNPS can be as high as +100 (the absolute best) or –100 (the absolute worst). Intuitively, anything below zero is cause for concern.

In Performance and Retention – Overall Turnover

Measures the rate at which employees – employees that you then need to replace with new hires – leave your company. These departures can be voluntary or involuntary. Turnover usually catches teams off guard, especially when employees leave on their own. It also requires hiring managers and recruiting teams to invest time and money in seeking a replacement.

Turnover Rate = (Total Departures ÷ Average Headcount) × 100

In Performance and Retention – Voluntary Turnover Rate

Go one step further in your retention analysis and look at only those who are leaving on their own, instead of you asking them to depart. This shows how many employees are unhappy enough that they chose to leave.

(Total Voluntary Departures ÷ Average Headcount) × 100

In Performance and Retention – Employee Performance

Going through a performance review cycle will give you great insights into who your top performers are and who needs improvement and why. Go one step further to conduct 360-degree reviews to help managers get feedback on their leadership and development styles. Cross data about your top performers against other key metrics, such as employee satisfaction or turnover, to gain more insights.

Conducted annually, bi-annually, or quarterly

In Performance and Retention – Revenue per Employee

Measure how over- or understaffed your organization might be by looking at the growth of your revenue over time as you grow your teams. It's also an indicator of the quality of hired employees. This metric is particularly interesting to benchmark against others in your industry to see how comparatively efficient you are.

Revenue per employee = annual revenue ÷ full-time employee headcount

In Employee Development – Career Path Ratio

As your company grows, this metric measures your company's share of promotions versus lateral moves. Knowing your company's career path ratio can inform long-term workforce planning and help you identify employee development roadblocks.

Career path ratio = total promotions ÷ (total transfers + total promotions)

We spoke to a number of CEOs to get an idea of the most common metrics that CEOs say they value. Turnover rate, engagement, reasons for termination, time to fill were all in their top five. Understanding these measures and being able to get down into the weeds on them can be of enormous value to organizations. – all mapped to business priorities that directly map to HR goals.

Take turnover, for instance. Seen as the "old faithful" of HR metrics, data on who is staying or leaving (and why) can provide an illuminating snapshot into what's working and what isn't at a company. Ethan Taub, CEO of Goalry (https://www.goalry.com/), told us the following:

> Turnover is a huge indicator of how well your company is recruiting, retaining, and improving staff . . . There is a lot of competition in business these days, and companies have to sell themselves just as much as candidates do.

Engagement surveys and exit interviews can provide similar glimpses into the company culture, as employees are experiencing it. These tools allow organizations to better assess any adjustments that they may need to make. "The feedback given, good and bad, can allow you to assess if and what needs changing for the better," Taub said. Engagement data should inform and empower employee engagement goals for the year. If you're hoping to improve company culture, these data points will give you the rationale to prioritize programs within your executive team.

Say you get a sense that diversity and inclusion are a problem at your company. Companies that don't prioritize diversity not only contribute to longstanding unfair barriers facing BIPOC and LGBTQ job candidates, but they're also hurting themselves, and making it harder to pull in talent. Mikaela Kiner, CEO at Reverb told us the following:

Diversity information on all fronts warrants your attention. That means your diversity of candidates, interviews, hires, promotions and pay increases . . . Lagging in any one of these areas will negatively impact not only your company's diversity but your ability to attract and retain diverse hires over time.

How can analytics help you address the issue? Survey data can help you assign numbers to the problem, putting it in perspective for executives who can increase the budget for additional training, invest in partnerships for more diverse applicants, and a host of other initiatives.

Of course, there are other metrics that you can measure, including performance and employee growth. But again, the specific data you cull together will depend on your needs and goals as a company. One thing to keep in mind when trying to decide what to measure: Similar to engagement survey results, you should try to limit what you measure to what you can act on. If a huge priority for your next two quarters is high growth and hiring, be prepared to track key recruiting metrics like Time to Hire. If your company is having a retention problem, focus on engagement metrics to measure where folks are unhappy. Then you'll be able to quantify HR strategies both to show value and drive business outcomes.

Gathering this data and pulling insights will help you build out a list of People team goals from quarter to quarter and year to year. When you have data across multiple aspects of hiring and retention, performance and feedback, employee engagement and satisfaction, and growth, you can cross these data points to make smarter decisions about how best to allocate your People team or HR resources – or whether to ask for more.

Of course, to leverage that data, HR professionals must effectively communicate it to the C-suite. HR can sometimes get short shrift at the executive level. But with hard numbers and data points, People teams can show how their wins lead to the organization achieving its overall strategic goals. HR professionals know that what they do isn't just something companies need to have for compliance purposes, as company leaders may often view it. People Strategy serves an essential strategic function, acting as a guiding light for organizations as they strive toward their goals. Data allows HR teams to quantify their worth, proving that they are as vital to an organization as marketing teams and sales teams – and, of course, deserving of a seat at the executive table.

Key Points

- Human resources should not rely on judgment alone – data can help people teams set goals, measure success, and inform strategy.
- Through data and analytics, People Strategy helps drive business outcomes.
- Data is the key to proving to executives that HR is a critical strategic function rather than a cost center that companies feel compelled to have.

Conclusion: The Power of People

Throughout this book, I've spent a great deal of time explaining how to build a people strategy by using my experiences with Lattice. And indeed, that is an important lens through which I see myself and through which I share these learnings. The chance to work with thousands of companies and People and HR leaders over the past five years at Lattice has been a source of learning, motivation, and fulfillment unlike anything else I've had in my career.

While the HR hat is an important one for me to wear on occasion (and one that I wear proudly), it's not my primary one. My first responsibility is to be the CEO of Lattice, the company, and to do everything that I can to make it the kind of place we want to help our customers become. Fortunately, there's a beautiful overlap between the work we do internally at Lattice and the work we do on behalf of customers. As the HR function becomes increasingly strategic over time, the roles and work of CEOs and their HR leaders are converging.

For the people in either role, the top priority is people – full stop. They're responsible for bringing great talent to the organization, setting the values and standards of work, giving people the resources and the space they need to be successful, making sure that people-related problems are addressed, and that people-related opportunities are identified. I feel very privileged to be working on something so closely aligned with the work I'm doing every day internally at Lattice to build up our company alongside the customers that we support.

Regardless of where you sit in an organization, 2020 has been a year unlike any other. But it has been particularly taxing on our HR teams. We had a global pandemic that completely upended the way that we work, and we've had to figure out what we want to be as companies going forward. We've had social unrest after the murder of George Floyd, and the desire to take a stand against racism and support our BIPOC coworkers. How do we respond in the face of a year like this? How do we stand up for what's right? How do we adapt and take care of the people around us? And how do we make work still feel meaningful when the world is upside down?

We've really had to dig deep and figure out how to transform to be the best version of ourselves and evolve our companies to live up to our values in a changing world. How do we respond? What does it take in the face of all of this change, in the face of all of this difficulty? After partnering with thousands of companies over the past several years while building Lattice, we've learned that, as company leaders and as people leaders, there are several important ways that we can respond.

First, *we must listen and adapt.* It's so tempting when life gets difficult to put our heads in the sand and hope that it'll all go away or at least pass quickly. But we need to do the opposite. We need to open our hearts and our minds. We need to open our ears and listen to the people around us so that we can adapt to the change that we're seeing in the world. Some companies are even incorporating "adaptability" into their company values, including one of our customers, Artsy.

"We actually rolled out a new set of values at the beginning of this year. One of our new values is 'transform together,'" said Gray Holubar, Artsy's associate director of People Operations during our Resources for Humans Virtual Conference. "We put a stake in the ground and said, 'Hey, we really do think that change is inevitable for our company and is core to our vision.' That's what we're going to ask all of our employees to be on board with."[1]

Now, I want to share a story about how Lattice tried to listen and adapt. Following the killing of George Floyd in June 2020, much of the world rallied together in protest. Lattice, as a company, had to decide: Who are we in this moment? What do we do?

We immediately stood up and said, "This isn't right, this isn't something we can stand for, and we want to do our part." But rather than simply deciding what that would look like from the top, we actually engaged the entire company. So, over 150 Latticians got together in a shared Google doc and we brainstormed ideas about how we could respond. What could Lattice do, and what would it look like?

Then, over the next month, we consolidated and prioritized those ideas into a concrete list of steps and goals. We shared what it was that we wanted to do, and we then published that to the world. As a company, all unified together we said "Here's how we want to contribute in the fight against racism." We could hear what we wanted to do together, to talk it through, and to make those changes as a company. And that included standing up for things like equality in hiring, pay transparency, inclusion in the workplace, donations that we could make, and support for education. And most importantly, we committed to leveraging our product that helps companies be more mindful of diversity, equity, inclusion, and belonging.

---

[1]Andy Przystanski (moderator), "Making Adaptability Part of Your Company Culture," webinar, Lattice website (2020), https://lattice.com/on-demand-2020-session/making-adaptability-part-of-your-company-culture

These moments will be different for different companies, but the key in these moments is to listen to the people around you and to adapt to the new world as it stands. And this wasn't just effective for Lattice. Companies all over the world were similarly affected. The act of listening itself is really powerful. When the coronavirus pandemic hit the United States, we ran a survey to thousands of People leaders, thousands of companies all around the world. And the data we got back was really striking.

One of the most interesting things we found was a piece of metadata, which was that People teams who used employee engagement tools felt more prepared for the pandemic. They felt more than twice as likely to rate their team's reaction as either good or great when employee surveys or pulse surveys were used. What we learned was that it's not just what we hear when we do a survey. It's not just what we learn when we do a one-on-one. The simple act of listening – actively engaging people around us – can drive unity.

The second thing that we need to do is to harness hardship and use that as something to our advantage. We need to make sure that we take these difficult moments, that we take the things that are new in the world and say, "How can we find opportunity in the middle of this crisis?" It's always difficult, but there's always opportunity, and when things are hard, that's when we get a chance to grow. And so, it is critical to remind ourselves, and remind the people around us, that difficulty is an opportunity.

Harnessing hardship to strengthen your culture is easier said than done. When things get really difficult, it can be hard to be the one who helps the people around you to seek change, because oftentimes we're enduring our own hardships. But one of the things I have found – and so many of us find – is that by being there for others, by being the stable rock for the people around you, we stabilize ourselves as well. And when we do that, we're able to see the opportunity around us and to get through the difficulty knowing that following the difficulty, there will be goodness.

Figma is a really exciting start-up based here in Silicon Valley. They make design tools that allow designers to collaborate while building their software. And Figma did something that I thought was really special during the pandemic. CEO Dylan Field wrote a blog post about what was going to be important for them as a company, while they figured out what work was going to look like going forward.

One of the major points he made was to acknowledge both his own and his leadership team's limitations when it came to decision making. He wanted to make sure that people knew, "Here's the information we do have, here's the information we don't have. And this is what it's going to look like for us to make a decision." Vulnerability is always an important quality of leadership, and vulnerability in hard times is even more important.

The longer I lead a company, the more I realize that showing our authentic selves and reminding people that we're just humans doing our best is always key. Vulnerability is what allows people to trust you, it allows you to be truthful – particularly in a moment like this. If a CEO got up in front of their company right now and said, "I have all the answers, I know exactly what's going to happen," you couldn't possibly trust them. But by starting from a vulnerable place and saying, "We don't know a lot and yet it's our task to make this decision," leaders can build even more strength for their companies.

I'm a strong believer in the saying "a smooth sea never built a skilled sailor." And the challenging moments give us the opportunity to learn the hard skills to learn how to improve. If things were always easy, life would be calm and we wouldn't feel challenged, but we wouldn't grow. We wouldn't get the type of stress that we need to improve and to find growth in our careers.

We also need to focus on fundamentals. When things get difficult, it's easy to get distracted, to become reactive to all the new changes and troubles. But what's really important in these moments is to center on what's always true. For companies, this may mean centering on our values and those three pillars of company culture. For individuals, this may mean going back to the core things in our lives that we know matter the most. But whatever that means for you, when the world gets crazy, we find our power by finding our center.

Looking back over the last several decades of work, it was really common for jobs to be about little more than receiving your paycheck. "Work" felt more like drudgery for many people. There were a few reasons for this: first, we didn't have the technology that exists today that allows people to work on the more creative projects; second, the expectations weren't there; and third, companies had much more control in the balance of power between employees and management. In other words, they didn't need to take care of their workers.

But over the past few decades, and particularly in the last 10 years, this has dramatically changed. If we think about how people find fulfillment in their lives, employment and where they work has grown in importance. What used to be just a paycheck has now also become a community, a sense of purpose, and a place to grow. All of these things make work so much more meaningful for people. And the ability for companies to provide that to employees today not just makes the human experience richer, but it also makes companies more successful. It makes employees more engaged. It makes them perform at a better level. It makes people want to stay longer and do well for their teams and for their missions.

And so, when we think about the pillars of people management, what are those things that people want out of their company? It's our culture. It may be now a cliché, but culture isn't about ping-pong tables and snacks. If this year has taught us anything, it's that those in-office perks are the least important part of a company's culture. So, what are those core fundamental elements of the employee experience that are true no matter what? What are the things that over these past decades we've been building toward that gives us this richer work experience?

Let's review those pillars again. With purpose, you help employees understand what their work does for the company and what the company does for the world. And by connecting those things, those individuals will feel a sense that what they're doing is worthwhile. Then there's community – making employees feel that they're part of a group with high trust, effective communication, equality, respect for differences, and high levels of cooperation. Crafting a space for a community to exist is one of the most important things that we can do as people leaders. And finally, there's growth, which looks at "Where am I going?" beyond the present experiences to the aspirational long-term goals.

I wanted to end this book on a personal note about my journey in building Lattice and some of the moments that have given me the confidence that the pillars we tell customers to invest in to provide an environment of meaningful work for employees – purpose, community, and growth – are in fact the most important ones.

The importance of purpose first really hit home for me when an employee was going through a tough time. Our head of design is just an incredible talent. He joined Lattice as a full-time team member when we were just over a dozen employees, but he has worked with us as a contractor since Day 1. He was a friend and former colleague of my cofounder and mine, he was someone we both deeply respected on a professional level, and we cared a lot about him on a human level, too.

So, naturally, when he came to me one day and told me he was really not feeling good about his situation at Lattice, it was very unwelcome news. He'd been working with us full-time for two years at that point, had seen lots of ups and downs, and knew pretty much all there was to know about our company and our people. "I don't feel like I'm growing professionally," he told me, speaking frankly. "And what's worse, I'm not sure anyone here necessarily has the willingness or ability to help me."

There was more. "And my compensation is all right, but not great," he continued. "I know I'd be making a lot more somewhere else. This isn't the most important thing, but as long as I'm sharing how I'm feeling about my job, I thought I should share."

This was a gut punch. Someone I cared very much about, a person that so many others at Lattice looked up to, and who was such an important part of the company, was telling me in no uncertain terms that things weren't working for him. I started wracking my brain for the right response. Do I empathize and acknowledge? Do I probe with more questions? Do I start pointing out all the ways in which I actually did think he was growing, and the fact that he was surrounded by people who cared a lot about his well-being and career?

But I didn't have to answer. He continued on, with the clincher that helped solidify for me the importance of purpose at work. "However, I want you to know that I'm not going away, and we will find a solution to all this." I relaxed. "When I think about what matters to me in my work, it's Purpose, People, and Pay, in that order. Right now, people and pay don't feel great, and I don't feel myself learning and progressing nearly as quickly as I'd like. However, purpose is the most important thing to me, and Lattice's purpose is exactly what I care about. Making work meaningful, helping people learn and grow . . . that's exactly what I want my career to be about, and I see so many ways in which we're already doing that and so much potential to do it even more."

I wasn't sure what to say. Here was one of our most important employees at Lattice sharing a list of reasons why things weren't working for him, but then before I could even respond, telling me that it was all okay because of our company's purpose. That moment solidified for me the value of a clear purpose, and the importance of having employees who felt a personal connection to that purpose.

The second story I'd like to share is one about community, which I mentioned briefly in Chapter 1. Of all the many memories I have of building Lattice over the years, one of the most vivid for me is the moment I first realized that we were forming a community that went well beyond any personal relationships I had with other people at the company.

Our first office (after the tiny, one-bedroom apartment we leased until eight of us were cramming into the bathroom and closets for calls) was located in downtown San Francisco. It was a beautifully well-lit space with big windows, high ceilings, and exposed brick – 2,400 square feet of bustling energy. The office had two floors: a main area and loft that you accessed via a stairwell in the center of the first floor. At our peak in that space, we had 20 people downstairs and 10 upstairs, and when I tell you there was no room for any more desks, I mean it.

One day I was upstairs spending some time with our sales team. I'd been there with them talking about deals, laughing about mistakes we had made, and generally buzzing with energy at the realization that – despite the challenges – what we had was truly starting to work. While they kept laughing and talking and brainstorming, I grabbed my computer and headed downstairs to go back to my desk.

And that was the moment for me; standing on the top step, with a bird's-eye view down to the office below, and with the sales team buzzing behind me. Looking out on the main floor of the office, I saw people in groups of two and three behind computers who were highly engaged in their work, I saw people sitting at the lunch table, I saw pairs walking out of the front door to go on a walk.

Lattice's small but mighty team was a thriving culture and community. It was a place where people were passionate about shared goals, where they were building real friendships through shared experiences, and where there was a clear sense of progress and personal growth. It was a moment that gave me goosebumps, and it will always be stuck in my mind. It's the type of vision that you never believe you'll ever see when you decide to start a company.

How did we do it? When a company is small, things are simple. When you can stand up at your desk, look around the room, and see everyone who works at your company, a high-trust, high-alignment culture is easy. We could build this kind of community because we had a shared purpose; we had high degrees of openness and trust with one another; and we had a clear sense of progress, growth, and hope. Good company cultures often come naturally from that.

The challenge comes with making this work at scale. Building for community, growth, and purpose when your company is 100, 500, or 5,000 employees – can be done, but it requires ongoing, intentional work, and I hope this book has shared some tips and clues for how to go about that.

I want to end on a final story about growth. To me, growth is the ultimate centerpiece and foundation of a strong company culture. One of the beautiful aspects of any start-up is that it is constantly changing, even though its core philosophy stays the same. The values and mission hold true, but over time, just about everything else is up for grabs and up for debate. Growth for a company opens up more opportunities for personal employee growth than anything else, and it also scales the impact of the business, thus amplifying everyone's sense of purpose.

And, on a personal level, watching others experience personal growth is what it's all about. The moments where I step back and think "this has all been worth it" usually come when I have the pleasure of seeing someone make massive leaps in their personal and professional growth.

There have been countless stories of this sort of growth at Lattice, but one that sticks out to me is Alex, a key member of our own executive team. He joined Lattice when we were tiny, with just four employees at the time. He was Lattice's all-around marketer, and while he'd spent a few years at a marketing agency, he'd never worked for a start-up.

However, as is often the case, past experience proved to be a much smaller part of the success equation than effort and ability. He gave the job his all, bringing tremendous amounts of creativity, experimentation, and hopefulness. He got more done as a team of one than anyone I can remember. He built a website, launched digital advertising campaigns, set up email marketing, created a content strategy, optimized our site traffic, brought Lattice to various HR events . . . I could go on. It set a standard in my mind for just how productive a single person can be when they're properly motivated, energized, and unconstrained.

This person operated as an extremely high-performing individual contributor for over a year, until the company's growth required him to start building a team. There was no question that he'd be the manager of the team. Aside from his incredible performance and impact, he was also a caring and thoughtful person who embodied our company values.

As he started slowly to add team members, some cracks started to show. As a department, marketing continued to do great work. The team was small, and he hired well. As a result, both he and his team members continued to be highly productive. But his transition to manager was tough; most of his time was still spent doing what he loved and felt most comfortable doing: individual marketing work.

"You know," I said to him one time, "now that you have a team, management really is your first priority. And that will just

become more true the more your team grows." He sort of nodded, thinly agreeing to keep the conversation light, but I knew
the story in his mind. Management is overrated. We all just
need to get shit done and take care of our stuff. The work is
what matters.

As time went on and his team continued to grow, the issue
became more pronounced. People on his team felt unheard and
unsupported, and he saw hiring as a costly distraction from his real
work. Part of me appreciated it; there's an opposite failure mode
where people think the answer to everything is hiring and management and spend nearly no time thinking about the work itself.
But this was too far in the other direction, and it wasn't working.

And as his team size approached eight people, and as our
business scaled past 1,000 customers, it became clear that the
marketing team would need to scale in such a way that the leader
would have to be not just a manager but an executive. At that
point, I had to ask myself a tough question: Can he get there? Or
is my job now to bring in someone from the outside?

It's a common situation for leaders of a growing company.
Your people are scaling quickly, but your company is scaling
quickly too. Can they keep up? Do you prioritize the individual's
growth or do what you need to do for the good of the company? One of our values at Lattice is Ship, Shipmates, Self, which
tells you the order of prioritization in a difficult situation. But
although our value clearly states that the ship comes before the
shipmate, and many other companies try to operate this way, it's
still a hard situation.

One great advantage I had in this tricky moment was a high-
trust, high-care relationship with Alex. We'd already been working together for two and a half years, which in the context of a
small and growing start-up feels like a lifetime. Our relationship
went well beyond work, and in addition to spending innumer-
able hours talking about this company that we both cared deeply

about, we knew and were part of each other's personal lives as well. So, we were able to have a frank conversation. I talked to him about the challenge, and as with any ambitious person with a high degree of self-belief, he was not happy.

Eventually, after quite a bit of discussion and introspection, I decided to call off the plans to start a search for a new marketing executive, since he was a key creator of our company vision, values, and culture. And perhaps most importantly, he had one of the highest slopes of personal growth I'd ever seen. I was ready to commit to investing in him and seeing if he could get there.

But to do it, I needed something from him. I needed him to acknowledge the importance of what I was saying, to acknowledge the places where he had these gaps, and to commit to investing in himself. I needed to know that he knew his primary work as leading, not doing. The deal was simple: he would work with an external coach who was a successful marketing executive and work closely under our COO, who was incredible at developing managers. I gave him a year to grow and get himself to a place where marketing was driving the company forward. The decision was made, and we moved forward.

Luckily, the story ended well, and it turned out we didn't even need a full year. Eight months after the decision to stick with this person, he had so successfully reinvented himself that we proudly promoted him to vice president. By opening himself up to the need for change, working hard to improve, and getting the support he needed to grow, we got the best possible result.

While it doesn't always work out this way, early employees who scale up into later-stage company leaders are often the most effective people you'll ever have. Of course, you will need to bring in other leaders over time, but I believe you should bet on your own team whenever you can.

And, on a personal level, these types of stories are what make work meaningful for me. Meaningful moments aren't always easy or pleasant. Getting to this end state with Alex was challenging. But he got himself there, and I and so many others felt proud to be part of creating an environment where someone with great talents and efforts could grow themselves from individual contributor to an executive in just a few years. Seeing employees at Lattice grow is a clear reminder of why our mission to help other companies do the same is one worth pursuing.

What are the stories we'll tell about work in the coming years? Obviously, that will remain to be seen. But I can hazard a guess. Even if offices give way to remote workspaces, the need for great talent will remain constant. Even if virtual happy hour takes the place of the water cooler, connection between coworkers will always make for better work experiences. Even if the present uncertainty persists, a tight-knit culture will always provide some degree of steadiness. Whatever the changes, positive or negative, that the coming months and years bring, there is at least one asset that will never lose its importance:

People.

Appendix:
Turning Strategy into Action

Now that we've walked through the components of people strategy, how do you roll out goals, feedback, reviews, engagement surveys, and growth planning at your company? We've created People Program Models to help you visualize and map out a month-by-month plan that helps you get started.

Our models are largely based on the cadence of Reviews and Engagement Survey cycles as big moments, supported by supporting components (one-on-ones, pulse surveys, team updates, etc.).

People Program Models

Always start your planning around Reviews and Engagement Survey cadence and timing. This should be determined by the needs and speed of change within your business.

2x2 Model

If your business is just graduating from basic annual performance reviews, then transitioning to Semi-Annual cadence is a great place to get started. It's also a great pick for companies where:

Sample 2x2

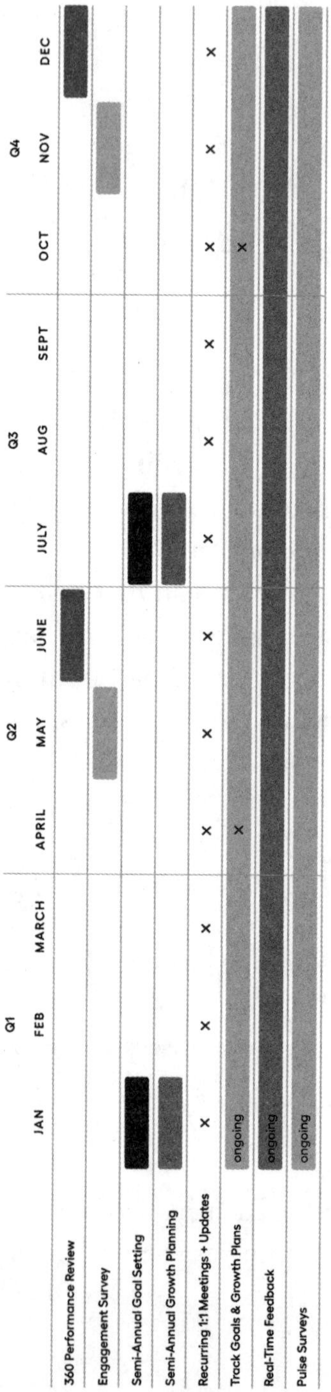

	Q1				Q2			Q3			Q4	
	JAN	FEB	MARCH	APRIL	MAY	JUNE	JULY	AUG	SEPT	OCT	NOV	DEC
360 Performance Review												▮
Engagement Survey											▮	
Semi-Annual Goal Setting	▮						▮					
Semi-Annual Growth Planning	▮						▮					
Recurring 1:1 Meetings + Updates	x	x	x	x	x	x	x	x	x	x	x	x
Track Goals & Growth Plans	ongoing			x						x		
Real-Time Feedback	ongoing											
Pulse Surveys	ongoing											

Performance Review: Fully 360 (self, peer, upward, downward) with scoring.

FIGURE A.1

- Business is growing at a relatively consistent, stable, and steady pace.
- Employee development moves more gradually and there's little turnover.
- Expectations for employees and managers aren't changing quickly.

In this scenario, companies would conduct two Review cycles – development in Q2 and performance in Q4 – and two Engagement Survey cycles (end of Q1 and Q3) throughout the year, plus two cycles of goal setting and growth planning.

To monitor progress and keep the conversations going, pulse surveys, real-time feedback, goal and growth-plan conversations, and recurring one-on-one meetings will continue ongoing year-round.

4x4 model

If your company is going through high growth where roles and responsibilities shift quickly and where teams have a high level of independence and autonomy, you should seriously consider going to a Quarterly cadence for Reviews and Engagement Surveys. This model is a great pick for companies where:

- Business is growing or changing at a fast pace.
- Employee and/or manager expectations are changing constantly.
- High growth and fast change could impact employee sentiment.

In this scenario, companies would conduct four Reviews – one comprehensive 360 Performance Review with quarterly

Sample 4x4

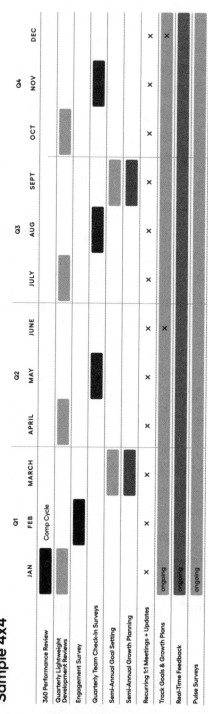

Performance Review: Fully 360 (self, peer, upward, downward) with scoring.

Quarterly Check-Ins: Efficient self and downward reviews.

FIGURE A.2

development check-ins – and four Engagement Surveys – one full baseline survey and three shorter, team-focused surveys. We also recommend two cycles of company goal setting and growth planning.

To monitor progress and keep the conversations going, pulse surveys, real-time feedback, goal, and growth-plan conversations, and recurring one-on-one meetings will continue ongoing year-round. If you're looking to aggressively build a culture of continuous feedback, then moving to a quarterly review cadence will certainly push you into becoming more advanced practitioners of this system.

Importantly, even though these examples are based on a calendar year, it's essential that you base these moments on your business cadence. So, for example, if you're a retail business and you're busy in Q4, then you should adjust your performance cadence accordingly (the worst thing you can do is to try and run a performance review during your busy season).

In the end, every company is different and will have its own methodology, so please just use these models as a starting point to build your own People Program system.

About the Author

Source: Jack Altman

Jack **Altman** is the CEO and cofounder of Lattice, a performance management and employee engagement platform that serves over 2,500 leading companies, including Reddit, Slack, Cruise, and more. Lattice was ranked no. 22 on the 2020 Inc. 5000 Fastest Growing Private Companies list and reached a billion-dollar valuation in 2021. Jack has spent over 10 years in the tech industry working in and alongside a range of leading global companies. Jack is a contributing writer for Forbes Tech Council, *Entrepreneur*, as well as a wide range of HR publications, host of the soon-to-be-released video series "Uniquely Led," and frequent HR industry event speaker.

Acknowledgments

I'd first like to thank my wife, Julia, and my son, Liam, as well as my siblings and parents, for giving me a high standard of happiness and meaning. Against that backdrop, I've come to believe that the hours we spend at work away from our families had better be meaningful too, which is an inspiration for this book and more broadly for Lattice.

Putting together this book required a great deal of effort, coordination, and insight from many people, most of whom are not me. Although my name is on the cover, projects like this always take a village, and so I'd like to start by sharing some gratitude for the people who made it possible.

First and foremost, I'd like to thank Annette Cardwall, who is the head of content at Lattice and was the driving force behind this book. After encouraging the idea of its existence in the first place, Annette played master of ceremonies for the creation of this book from start to finish. From helping to find the right partners for publication, advisory, and contribution, to editing chapters, to playing a key role in the overall direction of the book, Annette was the one keeping us on track and at a high standard of execution. Without her, this book certainly would not have come to be.

Also from Lattice, a big thanks to Luc Chaissac and Jared Erondu for their creativity and work on our book cover, and to our head of marketing, Alex Kracov, for his clarity of vision on what we wanted Lattice to stand for in the world and how we could bring that to life with this book.

A heartfelt appreciation goes out to our wonderful external contributors who shared their perspectives about leadership and management. This includes Marc Benioff (CEO of Salesforce), Heather Doshay (VP of People at Webflow), Courtney Ellis (VP of People at Anaplan), Nathalie McGrath and Anabel Lippincott (founders of People Design House), Daniel Chait (CEO of Greenhouse), and Dave Carhart (VP of People at Lattice). This group of people have been major influences on our thinking about people strategy, and their stories brought many of the points we touched upon in this book to life.

A special thanks to Eric Lutz, who spent many hours advising and consulting us on the writing of this book. His work was an invaluable part of making sure our key ideas were captured and that the writing was consistent and engaging.

We're grateful to Wiley, who greatly exceeded our expectations from a publishing partner. Their team worked closely with Lattice on creative guidance, project management, and final editing in order to end up with a result we can feel proud of.

Finally, I'd like to thank members of Lattice's leadership team, who've built the foundation for the practices and ideas over the years around how to build high-performing, highly engaged teams. Over the years, my conversations with Eric Koslow, J Zac Stein, Dini Mehta, and many others have had an important influence on my ideas and convictions around what makes for a successful company culture. Beyond that, my colleagues at Lattice have made my years of working on this company meaningful and unforgettable, for which I will be forever grateful.

—Jack Altman

Index

171

Lattice

Additional Lattice Resources

Looking for more resources to continue to build your People Strategy?
Check out these additional Lattice guides for more expert advice.

Visit [🔗 **lattice.com/ReadersGuides**] **for:**

**The Ultimate Guide
to Employee Development**

How to use job levels,
competencies, and growth
plans to make career
advancement crystal clear.

**How to Turn Engagement
Survey Results Into Action**

HR's guide to analyzing survey
results and implementing
change.

**HR's Complete Guide to
Employee Performance
Reviews**

Ensure performance reviews
are effective and impactful,
both for your employees and
your business, and create a
process with clear objectives
and less bias.

**How to Use Real-Time
Engagement to Build a
Winning Culture**

A better way to monitor, assess,
and improve engagement
across your organization.

People Program Models

Combining best practices across multiple organizational parameters,
Lattice's People Program Models help HR teams select a timing
framework best suited to the needs of them company — including
around timing for setting and reviewing goals, conducting
performance reviews, and running engagement surveys.

→ And much more!

Trusted by the best places to work

Join the 2,000+ organizations that use Lattice to
help power their People strategy.

lattice.com/demo